Perils, Tribulations and Family Values

Vincent Havelund

iUniverse, Inc.
New York   Bloomington

iUniverse books may be ordered through booksellers or by contacting:

iUniverse
1663 Liberty Drive
Bloomington, IN 47403
www.iuniverse.com
1-800-Authors (1-800-288-4677)

ISBN: 978-1-4401-9610-2 (sc)
ISBN: 978-1-4401-9611-9 (ebook)

Printed in the United States of America

iUniverse rev. date:12/10/09

Introduction

This is the story of a New Zealand Family the Mother is a full blooded Maori, and Father is an English businessman immigrant. They produce a happy healthy family, of four Daughters and three Sons; Father has died after being of great assistance to the 'Local Maori Tribe during and after the Great Depression'. Then the three Sons go off to WW 11 in Europe! One of the Sons is killed and the other two come home, but both are emotionally scarred by their experiences. The four Sisters get married and have many difficulties, as they settle in to life in Auckland City. The break from the traditional Maori way of life is very hard and with no males to protect them abusive marriages are made; only one girl marries really well. Finally Mother dies and chooses to come back in the Spirit to follow the lives of her children. The narration is simple and based on her love for her family and her eldest Grandson. The story is written by the eldest Grandson as a tribute to his Grand Parents and what they did when they fed the poor for three years free of charge, but in the process sacrificed their business.

There is also a series of short stories that are meant to give the background of the Grandsons life, after having been spoilt by his Aunts, Uncles and Grand Parents. In recognition of the family he loved so much all of the names are real, and the stories are written with much love to them all. Sadly at the time of writing all but two, the Author and his Aunt Clare are dead.

Index & Contents
Chapters

Author's Profile

The writer was born in NZ on Oct 25th 1935 and lived there until August 1970. He came to Australia before there was the need for a passport between the two countries.

He has worked in many industries as a Professional Public Officer for small companies for many years in both Australia and NZ? In early days that position entitled him to represent his client companies, at the Australian Tax Office and in the Equity Court of NSW? The Laws are now changed as the Legal Profession objected to that area of Law allowing none accredited practitioners to do legal work, which seems quite fair in retrospect? The writer did take accounting as a young man, but did not sit the final exams.

The areas of work that was undertaken has been numerous and created quite an interesting background, he has worked for many different industries over the last almost fifty five years? In NZ he owned and developed a very big wholesale meat company which failed for personal reasons after initial great success. It was at the time the biggest privately owned meat company in NZ; the loss when the companies as a group failed was large, financially and personally?

The industries he has had interests in were: Mixed dairy farming, Meat, Timber Soft and Hardwood, Fat Lamb Export, Heavy Interstate Transport, Mushroom Farming, Truck Stops and Restaurants, Professional Public Officer, (Australia only) International Finance in USA, London, Sao Paulo Brazil, Vienna etc; Shearing (NZ Only) Union Rep (NZ only) Canning of Tuna Fish, (Fiji only) Property Development, etc. The above interests are the source of the many short stories Vincent has written, from Humorous & Timid to Serious the vein is always, quick snatches of a very diverse life all in camera?

Year: 1914
Place: Kaitaia, New Zealand.

From a mixed Maori and Pakeha (white European) marriage, seven children are born. They are a very loving, happy family, father is a successful business man and mother nurtures their children to maturity, then at the age of fifty-four years of age, the loving husband and father Arthur, dies.

'In those years before the great worldwide depression Kauri Gum is used as a resin in paint and was mined mostly by the Maoris and a few Chinese prospectors, they were referred to as gum diggers.' It was a hard life, but there was no other work in the area. Farming was starting but that was at best a means of feeding a family, 'meat and milk production had not yet become the main local industry'. There was a fair amount of 'logging of Kauri timber for export as spas for ships and for local construction, but that too was in its infancy'. The gum was normally bought by the local agents for Australian firms and periodically what had been bought was shipped to Australia, flax was also a product the buyers needed again for the Australian market.

The death of Arthur (the father) in 1938, was the first change in the family group, and even though his sons carried on his business with the eldest one in charge, the start of WWII was not only going to interrupt everyone's lives' further but throw it into chaos. 'Change was only at the beginning.' The family intentions were changed further when the three sons enlisted into the Maori Battalion, even the youngest who had just turned seventeen, joined up.

This story is based on their Mother; (Mary) and her death as well as her decision to come back in spirit form to look after her offspring after enrolling in the Lords Spiritual army. We follow her spiritual work with her children in her efforts to help them sort their sinful lives and prepare them for their own entry into Heaven.

The work is very difficult and the mother is shocked at how much work she has to do to save her sons so they can gain salvation, through change in their life styles and to repent their sins. There is no special religious affiliation recognized, only the Jews are separated and expected as the chosen ones to live by their strictest laws is a part of the story. Reincarnation is an obviously strong part of the story as the mother works for her children's Salvation.

All other religions are ignored, Salvation is based on repentance of sin and the religious barriers of man are seen as just human created obstacles between our Creator and his favored creation humankind.

The story is about the life of the seven family members plus one Grandson who has been reared as the youngest of the family, and was seen as a son who under normal circumstances would have been legally adopted. The fact that he was not is the difference between the Maori cultural tradition; in which the raising of the grandchildren by the Grandparents is natural and accepted and Pakeha (European) law which can create legal problems.

Reincarnation is central to the books theme as is the spiritual war, with Satan's demons trying hard to keep their victims under their control. Christ's Warriors must fight equally hard to save their loved ones. The organization of Christ's army is far superior to that of Satan and the final victory is certain, but it only reinforces the victory Christ won on the cross at Calvary. The fact that every time one of Satan's army if beaten in a straight fight with one of Christ's army that losing demon is destroyed this is why the end is inevitable.

Chapter One

———◆·◆·◆———

The Book

Mary Stephens, nee Roberts: 1916 North Auckland, New Zealand.

Mary Roberts, a young Maori woman had just been widowed at the young age of 24. Not only had she been left a widow but three of her four children had died as had her husband, from the dreaded White (Pakeha) man's disease tuberculosis. Her one surviving child a girl; was sickly and it looked as if she would become a victim as well. Mary felt no great loss at the death of her husband; he was a brutal man; but the loss of her children was devastating! It was in the far North of Auckland and at that time a lot of change was going on, the whites had come in great numbers from all over the world, bringing with them their diverse cultures; but making no difference to the Maoris. The newcomers were all the same, all they wanted was land, land and more land, they people all wanted land for themselves. They had no idea of sharing; they wanted the land they had made their own, fenced so they were able to say; this is mine! You fellows stay away! Some of the local people agreed to sell, some did not. All the really good land seemed to get sold, and the poor quality land stayed with the Maoris. The land court had been set up in conjunction with the Treaty of Waitangi, but it was all pretty strange to the local Maoris. Many were happy to sell, some refused, but most didn't realize selling would alienate them from their land forever.

The future would see develop a strong dairy industry for cheese and butter, and a farmer's meat works would be built one hundred miles south of the area at Horotui. The meat industry did not become viable, until the first frozen meat ship was built, in early 20ᵗʰ century leaving Dunedin and heading for England. That method of sending the meat soon after that first trip became a great success. 'The more Whites came the more of their sicknesses came to the Maoris with them,' strange diseases they had never experienced before; it was really serious. The Maoris began to die off in large numbers, once they caught the sickness very few recovered.

The white man did not seem to be affected so badly, most seemed to recover and carry on, but for the Maoris it got worse and worse. The white men did not have enough women of their own, so they started to take Maori women for themselves, and soon there where cross breed children everywhere. But these children seemed to be stronger, they did not fall ill as quickly as the pure bred Maori children, they had obviously inherited the best of both races. As time went by they became known as 'Tarara's half bred Maoris and Delhi's, (or Yugoslav's)' these Tarara's were a striking looking people and the affinity with the Maoris was very strong. 'The was a strong tendency to breed back again to the Maori, and so there developed a strong cross breed peculiar to the far North, between the local Maori Tribes the Ngapuhi and the Yugoslavs.

The time was just after the World War one in Europe and before the great depression of the late 20s early 30s; times were quite good in the North, but not so good for this young Maori woman. Mary Roberts. Mary was born in 1890 and had married young to a Roberts, but it was a very unhappy marriage. Her husband was a drunken wife beater, a cousin, who was never at home except to breed kids and that was not very productive anyhow. By the time she was 24 years old Mary had had four children, only one of whom survived to be older than six years of age, all had succumbed to the dread Pakeha (white man) disease tuberculosis. Only one eventually managed to survive until the age of eighteen after which time, she also died of the disease. 'Mary's husband also passed on leaving her alone and distraught, with the one sickly daughter Harriet'. Not that the husband was much loss to Mary she hated him with a vengeance, and was left free when he passed on. She was finally free of the constant beatings that she had been getting, for the entire period of her marriage.

The real problem Mary had was that she had become separated from her own people, a people who she felt had not supported her during her brutal marriage, and from whom she dreamed of being released. She had grown cold towards them because of that very, brutal marriage, and had developed a burning desire to leave her own tribe.

The death of three of her children with a surviving one left was almost more than she could bear. The times were good, but hard for a young widow and certainly within her family and tribe, it was well known she was very unhappy and because of her brutal marriage, not likely to marry another Maori. Mary did not like her own culture; she was especially averse to the Maori funeral tradition. Mary proclaimed that dislike to her family, for her entire life. Mary was an extremely attractive young woman about 5ft 4inches tall, fine build and very sharp featured for a Maori, in fact if it was not for her color she would have been deemed a Pakeha.

Mary was full of vitality maybe too much so, and she would have no part of the many suitors that flocked to her door, they were dissuaded quickly and easily. There were in those days, weekly dances, and men would line up to dance with Mary, but none were able to get even close to her, she made it plain she would have nothing to do with any Maori suitors. Many were the young men who came a trying, and many were those who told bizarre and silly stories, but the truth was, that all were rejected quickly and with no compunction. Mary was not a frivolous person; life to her was very serious and she longed to get out of the condition in which she lived. Harriet the only surviving child was weak and sickly, and at that time, life did not bode well for a young very attractive female with no real roots. Every week was the same routine many were the men who tried their luck, both white and Maori. There were many Pakeha suitors around as well as Maori, but all got the same result. Thank you, but no thank you! This continued for over twelve months and then one day a new fellow arrived, he was a white man; quite presentable but very shy, certainly too shy to join the queue for Mary. He never went near her! He had asked every other eligible girl to dance, except Mary. Oh dear! What was to be done? Mary was smitten, but he never came near her! She could not think how to attract him; and wandered if in fact she was going to forever be ignored. This failure carried on for several weeks with Mary being about the only one not invited to dance by this new man, she was distraught! No matter how she tried to attract him she failed, he did not seem to notice she existed.

She found out his name, was Arthur Havelund Stephens. He was English, six year older than her and a business man. The drama really started when Arthur began to get serious with a girl Mary knew, and Mary began to get desperate. The other girl was making it very obvious that this Pakeha was hers, and there seemed to be a lot of merit in her ill concealed triumph, all the other girls withdrew and seemed to be saying 'ok he's yours'. But not Mary she would have none of that, he was hers the only problem was he did not know it yet. Arthur a poor dancer as with most whites, but he was a very personable fellow and very popular with the Maoris both men and women. He was reputed to have a special love for the Maori people, and went out of his way to be with them, 'he had arrived as a free immigrant having paid his own passage with no govt grant?' He was already set up as a trader with a general store in Waihopo the local trade area, not that there was much of an area, only Arthur Stephens and his store. Arthur bought, sold and traded; he had a good variety of trade goods and he bought flax and Kauri Gum from any who had those products to sell, that was Mary's opportunity? Mary had gum for sale, not a lot but enough, so she went to trade with all her female wiles well honed. 'Mary was after Arthur and he had better take notice,' well she hoped he would, so it was with her saddle bags on her old horse loaded with gum, Mary was off on her adventure too the Waihopo store. When she got to Arthur's Store it appeared deserted but the door was open; so she figured he must be around. While waiting she spent her time snooping around, she looked at anything and everything she was so absorbed she did not notice him come in until he suddenly said in Maori. Hello! How are you?

Mary got a surprise, she almost forgot herself and what she was doing, she was there to trade gum so, recovering herself she coquettishly stated her needs and invited Arthur to inspect her gum. Arthur was agreeably surprised and inspected her gum quickly; to her amusement it was very obvious he was very aware of her femininity. Mary now had the upper hand so she said; "I often see you at the dance, but you never see me?"

'To her surprise he said, "Oh I see you all right,' and so do all the other young men in the hall; I cannot compete with that crowd. Have you not noticed? My dancing is not as good as the young Maoris at the dance'"? Mary's heart skipped a beat, "really?" She said, "I thought maybe you did not notice me?"

To the contrary, with a smiled, he said, "who could miss you? I just don't like the odds; you are a very strongly pursued miss; and I am only a store keeper."

Mary's heart kept skipping in time with her thoughts, so in a rather forward manner she said, "why, I would love to dance with you, why don't you ask me?" "Would you dance with me?" Asked Arthur, rather naively as he took the bait.

"Well why you don't ask?" said Mary.

"OK I will," said Arthur with a happy smile, "I certainly will, but don't turn me down when I do will you!"

The following Saturday at the dance Arthur came straight to Mary and they danced all night. Mary was elated; and now it was her turn to be possessive and she did so with decorum, but with a steely resolve; this was to be her man and she let everybody know. The girl who had now been passed over looked very upset, but Mary didn't care about that she wanted this man for herself.

Arthur however was no push over, he was after all 32 and had been around a bit, Mary had had him take the bait but he had not swallowed it yet that was a wee way off, but no problem. Mary knew what she wanted; and that was Arthur Stephens, in the way of a woman she hooked him gradually while letting all and sundry know she wanted him, and all others should keep away.

Arthur was a very astute business man and he had proved that very quickly, his was the most important trading station in the far north. The local people came from everywhere for trade goods which he had in abundance.

His terms were fair and he was never known to cheat, his reputation was without peer in the trading stations of the far north.

Mary wanted a husband, but Arthur seemed in no hurry for that, so the problem was how to hook a shy Pakeha. That was not easy with a fellow like Arthur he took no leniencies and treated her well, in fact was the epitome of English decorum. This was not what Mary wanted so she began to go and help him in his shop much to his delight, she made herself almost indispensable but still no commitment, he was a real gentleman always. Mary began to wonder if something was wrong maybe he did not fancy woman or some other outlandish problem, and then one day none too soon she got the answer she had been waiting for.

Arthur started by saying; how lonely he was. Back home he used to attend church and mix with his peers attending its many functions, but here there was next to nothing. There was he explained no church that he had been attending and he missed his friends at the church he had attended in England. Every weekend he Sunday was a day we all looked forward too when we all got together. It was great if it was not for that companionship, everything in life that's needed would be here in this his new country

"What denomination are you?" asked Mary and her heart really raced when he replied: "Presbyterian, why?"

"Why so am I, we are the same we have a little Church I go to every week the sermons in Maori, but that's not a problem for you will you come with me? You will like our group and the minister is good he is a European, but fluent in the Maori language you will enjoy his sermon," she said hopefully.

"I sure will! It will be a pleasure to come and it will be so nice to get to know a Christian group once again, it's been very lonely until now," answered Arthur with a big smile, "you don't know how pleased I will be to go to the house of the Lord again, it's been so long and I miss it so much it really is all I need; to be at home in this my new country?"

Mary was overjoyed as she rode her horse home that day, she knew she was right here was the man of her dreams, and he worshipped the lord in the same way as she did; it was like a dream come true. Mary was in a hurry to get married the loss of her children and the sickly health of her daughter worried her, she knew Harriet was going to die and she ached for a new family. The fact they would be half European was she knew, the chance her new family would be better able to withstand the Pakeha's diseases.

The next dance was on the coming Saturday night, and when they parted after having danced all night, not giving anyone else a chance, she said; see you in the morning at Church!

He responded with a radiant smile and said, "You could not keep me away I will be waiting for you."

Mary had already explained to Arthur where the little church was, it was a dream come true for both of them. That little church with its congregation of about eighty reverberated with the singing that is synonymous with a mainly Maori congregation; there were a lot of Whites there too, because a lot of them were fluent in the Maori language as was Arthur. The interesting thing was the ease, with which the new settlers learned the language,

'Mary's efforts to learn the white man's language was slow and for her very hard, she never spoke Maori to her children but, always spoke English with a heavy accent.' Mary floated" out of the Church that day, she knew then it was only a matter of time and the shy Arthur would ask the question, and she was right. Only a week later he did, the old fashioned way a real proposal. They were married within three months and a better partner and happier marriage, she could not have wished for.

At the wedding Mary was radiant she had decided she liked this Pakeha's wedding ceremony, and wearing a wedding ring she thought was a wonderful idea. Arthur for his part looked so proud of his new bride and it was the best day of his life as he was happy to tell all of the many guests.

As it often was with Maoris of that generation Mary had her own land, it was quite usual for small pieces of land owned by a family sub tribe, to be transferred to a family member; this was the new way of the Pakeha.

Mary and her first husband had bought a five acre block when she was first married. Marriage in the Maori culture meant moving in to live with your partner, there was no formal ceremony. Arthur built an English style two roomed cabin and they moved in full of hope, and with a heart desire for true happiness it turned out to be a marriage built in heaven! Arthur was a busy man, but not so busy he could not always have time for his new wife, and he ran his business as well as spent as much time as possible at home.

The first big event since their marriage followed nine months after, their first daughter was on the way, and there was great excitement. Millicent Stephens a bonny girl 7.6 pound was born a really healthy child, both parents were delighted and the child was greatly loved. Mary settled in to build her nest and Arthur added a room to their small cottage. It was 1917 and their world looked good. The market for Kauri Gum in Australia was booming and the gum diggers were bringing in good volumes for sale, but the area was not a good one for flax.

Arthur's business was booming he was sending gum away every month and his general trade was very good, his customers came from long distances he had become so respected by all of the Maoris' and new Pakeha settlers.

The war was over in Europe but it had little effect in the far north of NZ. "Who cared what the Germans, French and English did to each other" they used to say let the whites kill each other the Maoris' had officially refused to send any men.

The war was a world away. A few of our boys (Maoris) had gone to the front but the Waikato people were refusing to send troops. The Member of Parliament Apirana Ngata was stumping the country trying to stir up support for this white man's war. In the far north that cared we were far away and Mary was in her own paradise. Unknown to Mary at that time in WWII the Maoris' would send a full battalion, and she would have three sons go to war, one would be killed and never return home.

Mary had her husband who she respected and loved she was free from those Maoris, she was learning to speak English; blow those plurry (bloody) Maoris anyhow she used to say. For the rest of her life Mary never spoke Maori unless she was with another Maori who spoke no English and she had no choice but to speak Maori. The problem was she never taught her children to speak their native language; even Arthur never spoke Maori to his children.

Mary had her own pigeon English and it was always a laugh when she let loose with an angry tirade in her broken Maori English.

Then the next child was coming and Mary said, "This one is a boy look how low he is in my tummy."

"Let's wait and see shall we," said Arthur.

It was a boy, Dick Stephens a bonny boy and he grew to be the leader of the pack. Next came another boy! Arthur was flat out building his business and building another room, he had no time. Mary just kept having more children, this time it was Darby. Arthur has barely time to blink and another one was coming Winifred.

It was 1920 and the war was well over. Mary was just getting into her stride, wow, another one Arthur was dazzled. He was getting a family all right, and a prouder dad one would never see!

'The more Mary produced children the harder Arthur worked, it was a wonderful family and Arthur and Mary were good parents. The family kept enlarging this time with the arrival of a girl; Anne Stephens in 1921, then in 1922 came Murray Stephens. After that there was a lay off time, maybe that was the last one, but no in 1926 came the last, Claire Stephens. So there they all were just as quick as that seven children; and Mary and Arthur Stephens were in heaven or so it seemed. The children were all very happy together, and they shared many happy times together, the parents as well as the children had a good life it was hard but worth the effort.

The house was built. The children were all born but now the future started to turn bad, not for the Stephens family they were well set up, but for all the Maoris in the north. The depression was coming and the good times were almost gone. All of a sudden there was no work anywhere!

Men were on the road looking for anything; hand outs casual work, just for food. Arthur's business was good he had everything; nice home, seven healthy children and a healthy wife. What more could he want? The only problem was the sale of Kauri Gum and Flax to Australia, had just about totally stopped from lack of supplies, very little gum was now being bought in by the diggers.

The year is now 1931 and it was really tough, the depression had arrived now and was at full strength, there was no work anywhere, and no money to buy any food. Arthur Stephens though had it all; his store was well stocked so he had nothing he could do. He went home to Mary and said we have been blessed by God. Now we have to give back some of what he gave us; we have to share with the less fortunate. Mary was in full agreement she knew how much the Stephens Family had been blessed, so she said Arthur, do what you must, we have had the good years now we must share our abundance with others. You are the head of our family so do what you must and we will all be with you, wont we children? They all agreed in unison that they should share their abundance with the less fortunate. This was done by Arthur giving credit knowing full well he would never get paid, but it was a way of sharing so everybody got a bit and it was all put on the tab, God's tab they called it and that's what it was the bank of heaven.

People came from everywhere to the far north, when it became well known there was credit with Arthur, and Mary Stephens. The family never abused or misused their creditors maintaining an orderly payment for goods received always until there was no more money to buy stock. It continued on until 1933 when Arthur ran out of stock for his shop, to his surprise, he found that he could not get personal credit to keep his business going; not even in Australia. So the shop closed down with nothing but a debtor's ledger, all chargeable to the Heavenly Bank. Even after all of that, it was a happy family, they had their home, nobody could take that it was on Mary's land, and Arthur had built the house with no debt so that's all they had, but they had a house of love with Mum, Dad, and the seven kids, until along came Vincent (Winty) Havelund Stephens, the first Grandson.

The Stephens Family became a byword in the North. Arthur Stephens was loved like no other, all knew what he had done and all respected him for it. The children were growing up healthy and strong a true family of cross breeds, they were a family of which to be proud of, but clouds were on the horizon.

As with all families when the eldest children are growing older and getting restless, the lack of anything in the way of entertainment was a problem. Suitable females for the boys would soon be a problem, Dick was old enough to be looking for a mate, and Mary had made it plain she did not want them to marry Maoris, so the field was very slim for her children. The eldest Daughter Millicent was the first to go astray, she had an affair with a Bobbie Roberts, but he was a first cousin. They had both betrayed Mary's trust and he was banished never to be forgiven. Millicent was sent to Auckland city to get her away from him, (Bobby Roberts son of a full brother to Mary) very soon after a baby boy had been born. Mary did not like Bobby Robert's and had barred him from their home much to Millie's anger! The pregnancy created a lot of tension in the home, Mary was extreme in her anger, and Arthur was quiet but hurt. Dick the most, he of all the children was most like his Mother; he was really setting up anger tantrums against his sister. It is not uncommon amongst Maoris' for grandchildren to be raised by their grandparents as their own. And so the fashion of the time this was what the grandparents wanted. The last one 'born in the family, 25th Oct 1935' and sharing the same birthday as Pablo Picasso was to be Winty's day and year of birth.

He was nine years younger than Claire and a new play mate for the young Aunt! Mary adored and wanted her first grandson for her own, and to be brought up by her and Arthur, but it was not to be. After Millie had given her word agreeing that Mary could have Winty for her own, 'she had changed her mind soon after getting married, and wanted Winty back'.

Meantime Arthur was starting to set his business up again and it was starting to grow, even though he still had trouble getting credit, but he slowly got the shop fully stocked and trading again. The family was digging for gum and so helping to bring income to the store, which was still the same one in Waihopo. Arthur was a loving man with a soft heart and the children all adored him, but he was not to live long. Arthur Havelund Stephens died in 1938 aged only 54 and he was mourned deeply by both Maori and Pakehas' in the North. Mary of course was devastated! The death of Arthur was the start of the family disintegration, Millie had already moved out; now Father was gone but in the end life goes on from what they all knew it had been everything moves on. For Mary this was a devastating heartache, but more was coming WW II was going to take away her Son's, the happy family life as they had known it, was coming to an ending.

Soon after Arthur's death' the Second World War started in 1939, and suddenly all the men were signing up to go and fight. The first one to do so was Dick, then Darby and finally Murray who was only seventeen years of age, in spite of Mary's protests he was off to war too. So the loving family was disintegrating and all that could be done was to shift to Auckland, which the rest of them did very quickly. Mary was left with just her girls one of whom was getting married and another three growing up, with a very spoilt grandson in tow.

Mary was growing ever closer to God her life became focused on the Lord, she prayed for her family one and all, and mourned the loss of Arthur. Then Mary was devastated with the death of Dick in Europe, and saw two of her sons return home from the war with emotional problems which she constantly worried over. Mary saw them settled and then slowly sank into a deep depression of her own. She loved her family dearly, but she missed Arthur and she was not concerned about anything now except Winty the Grandson. Mary's Family including all of the girls had married and settled and so she was comfortable with herself she proclaimed her Lord in her own simple way with her own simple faith. In 1952 she was went to be by Arthur's side. 'She did not go easily she had severe heart failure,' Mary would have wanted more time with her children, but she was at peace with her life.

Mary had lived as she had wanted, she was buried as she wanted; in the true Pakeha way in peace and dignity, she went to be with her father in heaven. The family buried Mary as she had always wanted in a simple Pakeha ceremony, and she was mourned deeply by all who had known her. Mary left a mixed breed family that was comfortable in the white man's world, but once the matriarch was gone the rest of the family did not stay as close as they once had been. Arthur was particularly well remembered in the Far North and his family was for many years also remembered. This was their way of showing respect and fond memory of Arthur Havelund Stephens, who had once done so much to feed the hungry Maoris, in the Far North of New Zealand. He had fed them for four years, and never charged them a cent.

Chapter 2

Joining the Lords Army.

It was my time to pass on and there was a full peace in my Spirit, but the desire to see my Winty more settled was very strong in me. As he stood by my bed my heart went out to him, he was losing his closest and only real confidant. My last thoughts as the children, all of whom including Winty stood by my bed, was of my children one and all and of Winty as a Son. Although my power of speech was gone, I signaled my last goodbyes with my eyes, but soon it was over. It was like going into a sleep and then I could see a tunnel towards which I was floating. My family were all gathered around my body, but it was time to go and I said my goodbyes tenderly in my heart, and left! Then I was coming out of the tunnel and could see a majestic figure all clad in white, and obviously waiting to greet me, it was a magical moment. I was in a gown of pure white and in total peace, I looked around for others but there was nobody. I was being greeted personally by our Savior and it was a stunning moment. Hello Mary he said it's so nice to welcome you, we want you to be happy with us and I know you will be. Love just radiated out of the personage obviously neither man nor woman, and so it was as a Spirit I now found myself, neither man nor woman. It was strange but there seemed to be no need to talk, it was as if everything was just understood, and it was all so perfect. Oh lord, I said, is there no one here to greet me? Is my husband here'?"

"Yes there are old friends and your husband Arthur is here and is excited you have arrived. First you have to settle in and cleanse yourself; all who enter here must first have been cleansed totally. Mary as you are newly arrived there are certain things that have to be done, before you can fully enter with your loved ones, but it won't be long," he said with a gentle smile. The Lord then led me to what appeared to be a church or house of God, and asked me to wait for a short while as my past was shown. I found myself in front of a pedestal and my name was read out from a very large book. As if in a dream suddenly as if in a flash, my life appeared before me from start to finish. It was truly amazing everything seemed to flash by, nothing was missed and some of the things that had been done by me were not good. There were things of which there was a feeling of shame, when they were recalled.

Suddenly there was a shout and my name was read out and I was proclaimed as worthy, a call of welcome went up, I was proclaimed ready to enter my new home! A shout of welcome went up and it was over, I was admitted into my new home and how glorious it was! It seemed that we did not walk, but floated within this new realm and suddenly there they were before me. Many of my beloved friends from the past, as if in a dream I moved towards them, they held out their arms to welcome me and it was if we had never parted Suddenly there he was before me, my beloved Arthur. As if in a dream I moved towards him, Arthur held out his arms to welcome me and it was if we had never been parted. It was so different though, we were apparently young and yet not so. It appeared as if we were ageless; time no longer mattered. We seemed to be in a suspended state and it was so strange and yet so good, it was as if all time and motion was no more. We had everything and yet nothing to do I was surprised but reassured by Arthur's ready smile; we did not speak just communicated, without having to speak. There were a lot of surprises when I asked for family members, I had forgotten a lot of them and only a few appeared, but no reference was made to others whom I had expected to make it into Heaven. Apparently many of my loved ones had already been rebirthed, by their own choice into one of the many options available to us all. It was as if nothing mattered and we were together again as we had been in years gone by. Of course some had failed the reception and had been reincarnated or sent to Satan's world. We did not believe any of them would have been rejected. And yet it seemed different and some surprise failures of missing loved ones was obvious.

Arthur and I were together and we were as one, there did not seem to have been any separation it was wonderful, Arthur was enjoying my presence, and equally I was enjoying being with him. It was then I became aware of how Gods Salvation worked? All on arrival home were greeted as I had been, and then taken to be cleansed or their life checked out, from the book of life. Those who passed the inspection were allowed to enter heaven to be greeted by their loved ones. The ones who don't pass were not allowed in, they were not given any choice and were compulsorily judged by God the Father. Those whose lives had not been too bad were immediately rebirthed without any choice as to their new parents. Those who were considered too bad in their past were ejected from Heaven, and became part of Satan's hordes. The interesting part was there seemed to be no consideration given to different denominations, as there was on earth.

The biggest surprise we got was the lack of fear that was part of our existence in Heaven. On earth there is so much fear generated by the different denominations, and the various interpretations of the bible. The book we discovered is symbolic and meant to guide, the killings etc are a part of mans free Will. The killing and mayhem that man has all around, and has had since Cain and Able, is a product of mans ambition and Satan's influence. The books of Daniel and Revelation that seem to Prophecy killing and mayhem, is a moving (changes with human development) prophecy, it tells us that man will keep killing each other and many evil men, will seem to be on the verge of dominating the world. We can see however this won't happen until the times are right for the return of Christ, and the Spiritual battle is bought to a climax. The wars as depicted in so many human examples are seen as between men in the natural form, we learned this is not so, it includes the battles in the spirit for the whole, Body Soul and Spirit. Only when the final battle has been won, and Satan's demons have been beaten will there be peace on earth, then all who have won a place will live on earth with fully reincarnated bodies. The New Earth and the New Jerusalem will be perfect, but only those who have achieved the right level of spiritual grace will survive to be on earth in those latter days. The reincarnation that has already been going on for thousands of years; has been the source for the building of the two armies, one Satanic and based on hate the other Godly and based on Agape (Godly) Love. These two armies are the ones that will fight the final battle, certainly at that final time the evil still living are to be destroyed. Just as will their spiritual partners all Satan's followers, will be destroyed as will his followers on earth. God's people will take control of the world, and those of his army who so choose will be reincarnated, and will be returned with imperishable bodies.

We went together to worship and to give praise, we were in a huge tabernacle with a mighty flock and we sang, praised and worshipped as one. It was a mighty gathering and most exhilarating, I could not express myself enough and yet I did not have to. We were a mighty host, but we were still totally individual. We expressed love for everything, love was the prevailing reality and enveloped us one and all. It seemed that we were in a perpetual state of love and togetherness for one and all; with our Father first? I found that there was no sensation of time everything just happened, yet we were kept busy all of the time. We did not seem to do anything we lived in a euphoric state. We were doing everything we have ever wanted to do but doing it with ease, and we lived in a constant state of giving praise to our Lord and savior. Often on earth the opinion had been expressed that it would be boring being in church all of the time and doing nothing but pray, this was not correct we were all very happy to be praising and giving thanks. There were a lot of other things to do, there were many of our friends who had not yet decided what they wanted to do, and were in no hurry to go back to earth, nor were they in a hurry to join The Lord's army. We are allowed to take our own time in choosing how long we stayed in Heaven, we are after all Spirits and quite unaware of time. There was not any problems with different language because we communicated by thought control, but if we wanted and spoke the language of the Spirit, with whom we were in contact we could talk to each other.

The relationship between the Spirits of different countries was interesting, there was no anger at all from those who on earth had been persecuted in their life time on earth. There was a happiness it was over and they could look forward to a better life when they were returned, because having won the right to be in Heaven they had the right to choose their future. A great number of those who had been persecuted on earth chose to join the Lords army; they wanted the chance to fight Satan and his evil army immediately. They knew they could if they wanted to choose to adopt different families for whom they could fight, and help their chosen ones win Salvation.

The big problem for our opponents as I found out later; was that when a Demon was defeated he was extinguished, and was no longer anything their defeat was complete and there is no return. In my later fight with demons in the lives of my own family, there was so much anger from individual demons whenever I won a victory, the losing demon vanished having been destroyed. The reaction from the demons still left behind was intense anger that was because one of their own kinds had been permanently extinguished.

I have no idea how long I was there because time has no meaning, we appeared to be in a state of suspension; there was no night or day. Then we were in a private hall in which I was to be interviewed. Arthur was there but he seemed to be in his own enclave and he gave me an encouraging smile, as I moved into the interview. It was as if I was talking and yet I was not. I was asked if I knew what I would like to do, did I feel I had a special calling and was there anything I would like to express. Many of my family had chosen to go back into the world and to be reborn; this choice was available to me as well as Arthur I was informed. Arthur had chosen to wait for me so we could decide together.

I asked that I would like if possible, to go back and work with my family the ones I had left behind. I came to know that this was indeed a high calling, but that if I wished this could be approved. I was made to know that the lord of hosts was indeed building his army in the world. A tremendous spiritual army was being raised, and all in the world would get the chance to know the risen God, the time would come when the Lord would return to claim his kingdom.

This time of Christ's return would not be until the armies were fully ready, both the physical one on earth and the spiritual one. Then Christ will take his place as the one and only leader on earth, and everything will be under his control. Christ will reside on earth in his full glory, and will be the focus of all those who live on earth with him. We need to understand that the world will be as it was in the Garden of Eden, but of course a worldwide Eden.

I was not verbally told anything it was if I knew what I was to do, and how I was to do it. I was going back to be a part of a spiritual army, which at the right time would be gathered together, and then we would inhabit the world bringing only love and godliness. We were going to prepare the way, but we knew it was far more than that. We knew that Satan's minions were not going to allow us to win the spiritual battle easily; it was to be the final battle of all battles. We knew we were in the lord's army, and so we would reign supreme in spite of everything that Satan could try to do to beat us. I was released to join God's army in the world of spirits; I could from then on come and go, as was needed. It was a little frightening feeling that the job that was to be done may be more than my skills could keep up to, but my confidence soon began to grow as it became clear to me what my job was. The priority was to be my own family, but there was also the freedom to work with other families, who in my life had been known to me and Arthur. The help we were to get was practical all we had to do was ask by way of prayer, we had to be very clear with what we needed and the help we needed had to be exactly as it is in the Lord's Will. All of us had a sound knowledge of the bible, and we were now imbued with the understanding that was not with me before. It just seemed that the in depth knowledge was now just a part of me, there was no need to think it all just came to me, it was a gift from God. It needs to be stressed though that only those who did know the Lords will, through his Holy Bible could be elevated to Christ's army in the first place. This was a battle that had to be pursued continually; we were to proclaim our Lord Jesus Christ throughout the Spiritual World. Until we were called we were to do battle in a practical sense, we were to try and protect our loved ones and to lead them to the Promised Land.

It all sounded so practical but in fact I had never known how evil the world really was, there was just so much happening. I had lived in an innocence that was now shattered in a big way, and I must say it was a moving experience. I found that Satins minions were indeed in control of the battle field, and even though we vied with them in every way, there were just so many of them it was a constant battle.

Arthur accepted my choice of returning to work with our family, but decided he would get himself reborn into a family he had chosen. We finally parted knowing this would be our final goodbye!

One thing about this job, it was easy to travel back and forth, but there seemed to be so many of Satan's myriads screeching and screaming everywhere. They were such horrible creatures, darting to and fro and enjoying themselves immensely when they had a perceived victory. I began to realize why the work I had chosen was so important to our Lord and Savior it was a very difficult one.

There seemed to be so much of a continual battle going on, it was obvious just how Satan was controlling the world, and how important it was the work so many like me had undertaken to do. The Lord had always had a large Army but now the spiritual battle was being joined in earnest, I knew there was so much to be done.

It was clear that many more were going to be allowed to enter Christ's army from after their entry to Heaven and after their examination from the book of life. The biggest shock though then was the big numbers being rejected for reincarnation, it was a shock. The level of strong evil among human beings is very severe, when we considered that many who were refused were immediately sent back, and yet so many were demonized to Satan's army. We calculated that only half of the new spirits gained entry to heaven, of which only 10% chose to enter Christ's army. Of the rest who were refused entry, over half were immediately reincarnated and the other half were sent to Satan's army. The truth was that far more spirits were condemned to Satan's army than were allowed to enter Christ's army.

The difference was that Satan's soldiers could and are destroyed; Christ's soldiers cannot be destroyed. Because Satan's army was so large, it was just amazing how many were rejected from entry to Heaven after their examination from the book of life. The biggest shock though then was the big numbers being rejected for reincarnation, it was a shock.

There is such a degeneration of values in this new world and the things we had taken as natural in our older world were being forgotten. It had been natural to have a Bible reading at the evening meal, and no one would dream of having a meal without giving thanks. These values were being lost in a changing world, it was so sad to see even as my own family struggled, so too did many more. It seems so strange that the simple truths of life we had taught our children so naturally were just being ignored, and actually forgotten. I thought of so many things that had been natural in our home and how love had enveloped us as a family, and yet so far I could see none of it in my children.

The ignorance and lack of knowledge exhibited by demons in every way was so different than we in Gods army had. We were it seemed now so highly attuned to the facts of life and our truth had become a shared truth. We understood automatically what was going on, where ever and however we received the knowledge. I don't know how, all I knew was we understood all things around us very easily. We knew we were in fact so attuned to the real thoughts of our savior, that it seemed we had a direct link to him.

An example of what I mean was the world news mostly coming out of America. We could immediately discern right from wrong and good from bad, but that is only a simple example. The media was quickly becoming an instrument for Satan; he was using it for the sexual abuse of the female body and the male minds. All dress was becoming sexually highly suggestive, and the sudden hugely increased appearance of homosexuality in the news forefront, was astonishing to many. Saying that sexual perversion had always been with mankind was not an answer; the fact that it was becoming so public was sickening to many. Many prominent people were suddenly declaring their perversions, and even same sex marriages were being legalized in many parts of the so called civilized world.

I had come back, had been to check up on all of my direct family, to be really honest I was in shock, having always thought Arthur and I had been good Parents. I was left to rethink where were we were at and what had gone wrong. Had we really been such a failure as it seemed, still the Lord had given me a job to do and I was determined to do everything I could to change my family; and bring them towards god's kingdom, but it was going to be a big job. The family no longer seemed to be a single unit, since my death they were neglecting the family unity that Arthur and me had tried to build up. Murray and Darby worked together but only because of the business.

Millie was alone none of the siblings ever thought of either her or Winnie. Of them all only Claire and Anne were very close and spent a lot of time together, Winty had left and was never heard from. How was I to move ahead! It was time to think. I had only access to the sub conscious mind; I could only work by trying to invoke memories. All of my life memories now had instant recall and I could delve into the past so the first thing to do was search back carefully. I started to do this but I was in for a shock, I had lived with the idea that Arthur and I had set up such a good example, memories started to flood back. Sure we had, had a great home but there were problems the first to come to me was my temper, always poorly controlled and always ready to let fly at any perceived wrong. For years my temper had been an embarrassment to me, now the results could be clearly seen the shame was all my own.

My language had been poor but did not sound so bad since it was cloaked in half Maori half English, so without much thought I could sheet home problems to myself. My beloved Arthur was never one to argue with me and he had left all decisions to me, so I was the head of the house. I had always planned and schemed to get my own way, and it was true always major decisions were made by me. Arthur merely agreed with what I decided, if he did not I would kick up such a fuss he would withdraw and leave it all to me, so there it was the fruit of our own misguided family.

I could see it all before me, and I could see the job before me was huge, and I had a long way to go. I spent the next two days in Prayer and meditation, oh lord I have such a big job to do give me the strength to do it, but I knew I had both his strength and his wisdom. I knew the job was big but that we would prevail, because in the end the Lords Army was in every way better equipped in the battle ahead, than our opponents Satan's denizens. The demonic hordes were huge in number, but where poorly equipped had poor leadership and in the end relied on sheer lust for sin to succeed, we had to break that grip to bring our people back.

It came to my notice our old family home in Waihopo was up for sale, and I knew it had cost Arthur and Me $1,000 originally and we had sold it for $5,000.00 in 1945. I had thought the price we got for the home was right because the 5 acres of land had been mine, so the price including my land was fair. I was shocked though when the home was sold again in 1955 for, $60,000, in my mind the price paid was obscene. What happened I wandered to the Lords instruction not to change the boundary markers? It was to take time to see and learn the effects of an ungodly monetary system that would bring the world of all classes into bondage.

The Lord's philosophy must win there is no comparison, but we must work to save our loved ones that is our war. Satan is well aware of the ideological reality that he cannot win, but he wants to destroy as many as he can therein, is the true battle. Our job to save all we can and so this is why we who choose to work with our families get such a high recognition, our job pure and simple is to save the ones we love and deny Satin his cruel aims, his job is to steal, murder, and corrupt though he knows he can't win that is the reality of the battle we are in, Love against Hate, Truth against Lies, the true Spiritual War.

It should not in any way be thought that Satan is in any way Superior; this is not so he has a place in gods' plans, but he is the real loser and he knows that is true. Satan knows what the end will be, since he was first removed from Heaven he knew the end result. The Lord's army would prevail; but there was to be a period in which Satan's army could be separated out from Christ's followers, those such as me who was there to fight for our families. The idea of reincarnation was that over a long period of time the real warriors for Christ would be separated out, those that were truly evil would be fully rejected and had no chance to find their way back to heaven, they would never enter the future true Godly Kingdom on earth.

This truth did not seem to be understood by Satan's followers, they seemed to find comfort in their numbers and to be convinced theirs would be the final victory. As we watched their, to us crazy antics we wandered how there could be so many who had lost their way and were following the wrong path. For us of Christ's army in general we felt only pity for those ugly brutes, but they returned our pity with pure hate, it was just so pitiful to see. We were all aware though that these demons of Satan's; had been the most evil of humans in their past lives on earth, so our sympathy was not justified. These demons had been fairly warned and properly judged by God they had fully earned what they were getting, fair retribution for the sinful evils they had been responsible for committing. It was interesting to watch the two armies in battle; Christ's army had the ability to ask the Holy Spirit for dreams, visions, and for the Spirit to communicate with their loved ones in sensitive ways.

Satan's soldiers could create pain with their claws and give evil visions while their victims were awake, they could not reach into the sub conscience by way of dreams in the sleep. They could not influence by way of invoking memories of their victims past, while the victim was sleeping. The pain they could cause when they perched on victims shoulders and dug their claws in as deep as they could was a very sorrowful thing to see, and we fought had to bring relief to their victims.

We warriors for Christ were communicated with constantly! I don't know how, it just happened if we wanted knowledge we only had to think and the answer came to us, if we needed practical help all we had to do was pray and we got the help we had asked for. As a spiritual warrior in the Lords army these are the truths we knew, and we could see the lord's hand at work as we battled Satan's hordes in the spiritual battle. It is a spiritual battle that is already won by Christ on the cross at Calvary, but the idea is to strengthen that victory, not participate in a mindless fight with the demonic hordes of Satan.

They are in no way equipped to win this fight because Satan's basic ideology does not work. Hate destructs and so Satan by the very nature of his work destructs, love constructs these are two opposing doctrines created by our Father which separates his children from Satan's children. Christ said we can only have either God or Satan as our Father, the descendants of Isaac or those of Ishmael. We found the symbolic separation of the two Sons of Moses was also with a purpose that is misread by the Christian Community. The separate of the Sons help define the sect or method of worship. Those churches that were directly descended from Christ were considered to be of the line of Abraham, Isaac, and Jacob; all others on earth are from the line of Ishmael.

The great multiplicity of different churches is not a problem, it's the abuse of God's children by the leaders of the churches that is a problem, and so hated by our Father in Heaven. Christ in the bible tells us to beware that we don't abuse his lambs; this is just what the leaders have done and are still doing.

Chapter 3

—◦·✦·◦—

Darby.

When returned to my Son Darby's home what a shock I was in for! His whole world was infested with demons, and they were not about to give up the battle field in a hurry. They enjoyed my humiliation as I watched the degradation of his beautiful family. Darby was now into his early forties and he had an unhappy life, the demons that were wrecking his life were Alcohol, Cigarettes, Extra Marital Sex, Business Immorality, I cried out loud for him but of course he could not hear a thing. It was a true battle as Darby went about his way living in all these sins. I was there to dissuade him, but to do this I had to defeat the demons in his life, and it was going to be a real battle.

One night Darby decided he was going to go out to party, girl friend booze etc the works, try as I might to stop him, there was an equally determined band of demons keeping him going. I was heartbroken as Darby wallowed in sin, the demons surrounding him gloated over every little thing he did it was a fiasco, but I determined to fight in every way I could to save my Son. Oh what a shock Arthur had been such a good Father to them all, and yet Darby was a mess.

Darby's eldest boy Andrew came in the next morning, while Darby was completely hung over and said, "Dad are you coming to our football game you promised you would today?"

"Oh no look here's $10.00 go and enjoy yourself," winced Darby.

"But Dad I don't want that I want you to come and watch me play!" said Andrew.

"Ok next weekend I promise." said Darby.

"Yes but that's what you said last weekend Dad are you not interested in what we do?" asked Andrew sadly. "I don't want money I want you to come to the game please Dad." "Oh go away Son can't you see I am tired?" moaned Darby. "Yes I know dad you're always tired when it comes to me I may as well not have a father!" said Andrew.

"That's not true I have just had a big night, look take this $10.00 and I promise I will be there next week, said Darby.

"Yes OK but I know you won't be you always promise, but that's all you ever do is promise." moaned Andrew. I just listened in shock and remembered all the games that Arthur had gone to when my boys were young, what had happened I could not believe it?

Then Dawn Darby's wife came in, "so what's wrong with you got a hangover who were you out with last night some cheap skate floozy I'll bet? And what time did you get home or have you just got home?" she asked.

"Oh bugger off woman said Darby; you give me a headache why don't you go down and see your drunken old Mum and Dad. You think you are so good, just buzz of and leave me alone." snarled Darby angrily.

Darby's demons were dancing in sheer delight, looking at me with sneers on their faces as if to say, see this is our household there is nothing for you here, true, I must admit things did not look good, but I was not about to give up without a fight. I tried hard to concentrate to get through to Darby's conscience after all what else was there that could done; I tried to remind him of his own Father. I was determined to get through to him, but it was not going to be easy, it was time to leave him for a short time, and went to his Brother Murray's house, fortunately he wasn't as badly off as Darby, well, not quite?

It was time to realize now the enormity of the job ahead I had to plan properly how to continue, it was quite useless to try and attack Satan's hordes. We had to be far more subtle than that, we had to get through where they could not, and they could not influence the mind, we could.

The Satanic influence was the satisfaction of the sin now; which gratified the senses, but left guilt as the after effect. To break the sin we needed to tutor the subconscious, and in this way counteract the lust for sin. I chose as my first challenge Darby, he was the one who seemed to be the in the most trouble although he would not have agreed to my prognosis, he was busy enjoying his sin hugely.

When the various NZ; military units arrived back from the war in Europe, an American unit was still stationed at Papakura military camp, and they were the source of much anger to the New Zealand troops arriving home. Many of the married man on their return had found their wives either pregnant or with small children, that had been the result of affairs with American's. Therefore a hatred of all American's ensued!

The Maori Battalion was back, and after all of the Pakeha units had arrived back a big march down Queen St the main thoroughfare of Auckland City was arranged, to allow the public to honor them. Then when the march was over they were officially to be recognized as having been demobed, from all military duty. The Americans had gathered in numbers and wanted to congratulate the Kiwi's, instead the simmering dislike towards them could not be controlled, and there was a fisticuffs battle royal that was the talk of the city for years. 'Nothing could be done because the fight was between Americans and civilians, none of the Kiwi's could be charged'. After he arrived back from the war in Europe, Darby had been just another soldier being released from uniform, but it did not take him long to get back to his womanizing and boozing ways.

Generally he did not drink or smoke as much as he did, but it had increased after he had been home for several years, still he always did like to be with lovely girls. He had been back about six months, when he came home with Dawn the eldest daughter of the family we had lived with when we first arrived in Auckland. 'We Dawn and I were both surprised to see each other, but it soon became clear her and Darby was a serious pair; they were married within another six months'.

To work with Darby I had to get into his memory, to find out what had caused his down fall? Where had it started and how had it grown so bad to do this I had to go back through his life? I remembered Darby as a boy always in Dicks shadow whatever Darby did, Dick could easily do better; it did not matter at what, then I remembered how without realizing, we were always applauding Dick. Poor Darby would slink away always second never the best; that was kept for Dick and so did the special applause. My heart began to ache as I remembered and then under stood what we had unwittingly done, 'Darby was the loser had always been and still was; he could not come out from under that shadow'.

How do I send a good seed into his memory? What created the slob he had become? Why put at risk such a beautiful family? There's Andrew, Robert and Cheryl, his children, as well as his marriage, he was putting it all at risk. Why was this so, how do we fix it? But then the real problem starts, Darby's wife Dawn starts an affair of her own with one of Darby's staff; and what a mess that turned out to be. When Darby found out, he was devastated but what could he say; he brought it all on himself Darby was the loser again. But it's really the children that lose, it always is, and that is the worst part!

Darby abused his marriage and he paid the price, he loved his wife and children dearly yet he was an adulterer. How silly! The children especially his daughter loved her father deeply. Yet he caused them so much pain, as I looked at the situation and knowing what a good heart Darby really had, it just staggered me that he had been so foolish. Andrew and Robert his two sons both served apprenticeships with the company, but he did not encourage them to enter management, rather he wanted Winty to take over the company. If he had spent the time on his own sons that he did on Winty, they could have taken over from him. It was all such a mess he loved his wife, and kids yet made such a mess.

Dawn had started a relationship with one of Darby's best friends; and the effect was unsettling for the entire family. All of a sudden Dawn was with a new man, the children were split up and Darby was on his own. Dawn remarried and it was over! Well up to a point it was, really Darby and Dawn still loved one another, but it was too late it was over and life goes on. Then Darby employed an ambitious house keeper; and he is up to his old tricks again, oh my very quickly. What a disaster, Darby now has a young wife, and a new baby daughter, and his new wife doesn't love him! Not in the slightest!

Meantime I am starting to remind Darby's of his youth and I am stirring up memories slowly, but he is starting to react. I manage to remind him of his academic success, and how he had won several competitions for writing; way beyond anything Dick had done. It was also true he was a better public speaker, the entire thing for which Dick had no taste. I began to stir his memory and get through to him in the only way I could. Slowly very slowly change began to take place Darby began to change his focus; he started to take interest in things he did as a boy; it was very slow but it was there.

I stirred his memory of meals and singing times around the camp fire; at which he was the lead singer, and how much we had all loved his voice. Slowly in his later years I took him back to his Father, and how well they had got on together, and then reminded him of so much more that had made us a loving family. Not one was separate, all were dearly loved, slowly but surely he remembered those great times. I could not remove what was done, but I could bring back good memories; and I could recreate in his mind things; that were positive and true.

Darby was the one with the best singing voice. Dick played the guitar and Murray was not interested, he could not sing a note. None of the girls were much at singing and Arthur and I were not songsters. Little Winty as a toddler had a beautiful voice, but he wanted to be paid to sing. Arthur used to be so proud of Winty said he took after himself. Winty if we asked him just loved sitting around the fireplace singing, especially if someone gave him a penny.

I had no memories of Darby's war years, and then quite unexpectedly one day some things started to come out, Darby was sharing with a friend about the war, and how he had been at the Vatican at War's end. I had no knowledge of this, so of course I listened to see if anything said could become a help, and in a way it did. Darby started to say how as a boy he had been reared as a Presbyterian; and how he had enjoyed the whole experience.

All of a sudden he started to talk of the Catholic Church, and how the Vatican sat on untold wealth, and left their flock to die in untold misery. Darby was suddenly aggressive against the church, mainly the Catholics. I had never heard my son speak this way before, and it was very obvious he carried a problem with the church as a whole, but the Catholics in particular. What surprised me was my children had been brought up Protestants; we had no Catholic background at all.

His listener was encouraging Darby to speak up and for that I was grateful, as this was something I knew nothing about. I hoped things would emerge that would help me in my search for positives, and it did all of Darby's previously un-stated disapprovals came forth in a verbal torrent, that I thought would over whelm me.

He spoke of the churches accumulation of assets that was not used for good, but locked up in the control of old men hidden faces he called them. He carried on with feeling, on how there was untold wealth in church assets, that were not used simply because there was no way it could be done. People left entire estates to their Church, and this became another unused asset of real value, but locked away from the world and suddenly of no real use. I was indeed surprised! Here was a Son of which I knew nothing, and I was so pleased for this opportunity to know more, and to hear his words so strongly expressed from the heart.

His listener began to take a different point of view, and pointed out just how much the church did within our society as a whole. His friend quoted the Catholic education and medical work, and he was strong in his support of the church as an under girding of our way of life. All of these things Darby very willingly agreed to, but he would not concede that the church net effect was a strong positive. Darby launched into a tirade against private medical and education which was church sponsored, but largely government funded. His argument was that the influence generated to the Church was disproportionate, and to the communities real cost; and therefore should be bought under state control. His friend then started to say that the Government system was already creating a senseless beauracracy, that had no control what so ever. It was an argument that was able to be carried on indefinitely because so many different points of view. All of the views expressed were perfectly legitimate were discussed, such as control of thought in our universities by the educated elite, but thankfully the discussion did not get into that; Darby and his friend agreed to disagree and parted.

However for my part I had a new perspective to work with and I was very excited, so I started to delve into my memories to find the source of thought that had triggered Darby's negative feelings towards the church, and all of a sudden it was all there. Darby had been inclined towards an academic career, but had been turned down unceremoniously by a church board of governors, on the grounds of Ethnic and Financial failure. I remembered the day well when it all happened, the exam had been sat and Darby had passed with honors, we all just took it for granted he was headed for a better education.

Then a letter arrived asking for the parents of Darby Stephens to attend for an interview with the schools board of Governors, I had no idea nor did Arthur think there was going to be a problem. We duly arrived and were ushered into the presence of the representative of the school board; it was immediately obvious there was a problem. Firstly as was obvious I was a Maori and that was the first strike out, the next thing was well what your source of income is. This was in the period where we had elected to give our income away, so it was a little pointless to say well it's like this, we are investing in the bank of heaven.

Church school or not this would have been greeted with some scorn; we of course had our home, but that was sitting on Maori land. Oh dear me! That was totally unacceptable as an asset; that was only a native asset. I now remembered the aftermath so very well. For the first time as a family we had been discriminated against, and how do you explain that to a teenager, specially one who was seeing his chance to prove himself being taken away so unceremoniously; it was a time of family upheaval to say the very least.

Darby swore out against the Church and as much as we tried to persuade him to desist, his anger against the church was loudly voiced, and now so obviously had become a poison within him; it was sad that I could have missed it so badly. What was I to do? I had found the problem, but how was I to fix it? I had to ponder that for some time but I knew there was not going to be a quick fix, no way in the world that would happen. I began to dredge back for happy memories associated with the church and there were so many, but I needed to be able to find a major event, one that would stand out but at the same time enfold Darby.

I could remember no such thing but I knew there had to be a happening, and then I thought it must have been when they were overseas at war. There had to be a church participation that was positive to the troops, it was an essential part of any war effort that trained clergymen would be on hand for them when their lives were in danger. There were numerous men who had risked and shared their lives with the troops. I had to find some reference to Darby's experiences in that area; I could delve into the unconscious, but it was very tricky. I needed a starting point; a memory flow needed to be created that was positive, but how could I find that? I could trawl through his memories and hope to find good results, I wanted better than that. I needed to have a point at which to start and then I remembered.

When our troops had arrived back from overseas I remembered Darby had with great pride, introduced me to one of the Ministers who had been with them right through the War years. Darby had said to me this minister saved my life in Egypt Mum, it was said with great pride and I knew I had the answer. Now I had to find and resurrect that memory along with a lot of others of course, this was not a small job; I knew I had a big job to do, rescuing my son from himself and it would take time. What I was doing was looking for the base from which to move forward, I knew I now had a good source of material; all I had to do was to start working with his memory.

Meanwhile Darby's demons were so sure they had a total victim they celebrated with horrible gusto, I could only congratulate myself I had not finished up as one of them, Praise the Lord I was in his Army. Oh Praise God! It is with horror I had to watch them celebrating every time Darby wallowed in sin. All of his practices continued unabated, his children all suffered the fruits of Darby's misdoings. They were all around him, his life was a mess and yet he continued to make it worse day by day; the more he sinned, the more his demons celebrated. For my part, how do you beat a mother's love? I was more determined than ever to save my son from himself!

I created for myself, a diary of his good memories and I kept them ready to feed them into his dreams. My intention was to have him going through a constant barrage of good memories, while dreaming. This was not really necessary because my memory was now so acute there was instant recall, but the diary was just a spiritual device, not a diary as it was known on earth. I wanted to keep up the pressure because I knew Darby needed constant attention, he was the one I needed to be with at this stage. I did not want to be working on him and having things slip while I was with one of the others. So my full concentration was on Darby.

Night and day I watched him and depending on what he got up to during the day was how I regulated his dreams; then when I could I inserted war time memories especially those related to that certain Minister. We were not able to work with several patients at the same time; we could only work with them one by one. What we did have is instant transfer to anywhere; if for example Winty needed me in America or anywhere it was possible for me to be with him immediately.

It was nice to see that so often now; Darby's mood was more placid, I would like to say his sins were starting to lessen, but that was not happening. Darby was still as dedicated to his sinful life as ever; and so often I felt like giving up, but that's not what I was sent for! I knew my job and I kept at it without stop, night and day. Darby continued on with his sins unabated, but I seemed to notice a lack of gusto, in his activities he did not seem so dedicated to his ways anymore.

I began to wonder if I was having a positive effect. It was too early to tell, but my hopes started to rise. One day young Andrew said to his father come to football dad, and I was delighted when Darby said sure Son I would love to. I knew then I was making headway, Andrew was so pleased I could see the look of appreciation in his eyes as he went out with his dad, I even noticed the look Darby shot his son as they left a little akin to what Arthur used to do to him years ago.

So I felt I was proceeding well! I thought my program of memory recalling were fair, because they were only his own memories brought back to him, I was happy that I was starting to get an effect; only a small effect but an effect none the less. Dawn and Darby saw each other often; and it was so sad really they were still so obviously in love, but it was over, nothing could be done. Only a few years later Dawn died and I was sure she died of a broken heart, what had started off as pay back; had proved to be more than she could take. When caught she could not go back, and she had no affection for the man she had the affair with, and later married.

I kept right on attending to Darby night and day, I never let up on him and he did seem to be improving, he did not seem to go out on his drunken sprees so often now, and he really seemed to be a lot quieter. As I watched him; Darby seemed to be changing within himself; he did not seem to be in so much of a self damaging mood; and he seemed far more reflective of what he was doing. I was unable to work out if that was because he was thinking of his past, reflecting on his future or maybe just in a drunken haze.

Anyhow I was determined to keep at him, I had started the work and I was not going to give up or even slow down. I was sure it was starting to work, and I could see the effects slowly taking place. The effects of the dreams I am sure were positive, and I was going to keep it up but I was equally sure, if I stopped he would once again sink into that sinful world of his own. I could see his thoughts were awake; and I could see the memories were stirring him, I was sure it was memories of such a loving childhood then when it was at war, I could see even those dreams were positive. I had by now worked out a definite routine for Darby, but it was still too soon to leave him; I had to keep pushing him and keeping him clear of all problems.

There was now a definite slowing down in his activities and I could see there was less Alcohol, I think his consumption was cut quite dramatically. He seemed a lot clearer eyed, and he certainly had cut down on going out womanizing, that part was very clear. His attention to his Children had improved immensely, and he seemed to be trying to copy his own Father.

I was so delighted; I wished Arthur was with me so I could share the pleasure.

The impact of Television was becoming so dramatic; it was as if the home was now being invaded by this media instrument. It had now become the "box" focus of the family or individual meals in front of, fall asleep in front of, and in fact, it seemed to dictate everything the family did. For my part I found it a waste of time, to me it was only rubbish anyhow, the time the children wasted in front of it, was a sin of the greatest order. The children insisted on watching so many silly programs, only when Darby wanted to watch the News, was there a break from the humdrum nonsense. On the other hand the news was full of negatives, there were never any positives showing, I often wandered just how far this was going to go. The new era of instant communication was just starting, I knew because I was tapped into Jesus; that there was an awful lot more to come. The king of the world; was going to use communication as a lethal weapon, in his fight to influence the minds of the people. The fight was getting more invasive to all mankind; it was so pleasing to be on the Lords team, in this mighty spiritual battle.

By now, my beloved Darby was definitely responding to my care and attention; day by day week by week, he was becoming more clear eyed; he now spent less time in the hotels and clubs more time at home. His clarity of thought was returning; he definitely was not going out womanizing. Losing Dawn may have been the cause of that rather than my work. But I was sure I was getting through; I had now to start to swing him in a positive way toward the church; that was next on my agenda.

I was happy to have been able to guide him the right way towards his childhood memories, which were paving the way followed by war memories; it was time to cut down my work load here and move on to Murray. I resolved I would return regularly to upgrade the dream program I had instituted; it was all going well it was time for the next work. Darby was progressing nicely and improving steadily, with the help of positive dreams, I was becoming truly heartened both of my Sons seemed to be progressing, but there was a really long way to go. It was going to take a long time to get to where I wanted us to be going, and that was a commitment to be in Gods Spiritual Army.

Darby was progressing quite well and only rarely "falling off the wagon", he was going out quite regularly with his Sons to sport, but he was still prone to alcohol and I could see that was going to be a major problem. When Darby had arrived back in NZ and de-mobbed from the Maori Battalion, he enrolled in the Government rehabilitation program for returned soldiers. This program was used to teach returned soldiers, new working skills and Darby elected to take up a carpentry course. This was a type of apprentice program except they were paid full wages in recognition of their service, it really was learning on the job. Darby had passed through the course and immediately gone to work as a carpenter for one of the major construction companies. During his first year he befriended a Jewish fellow who was older and had been a builder, in Europe before the war and had recently immigrated to NZ with his wife. The fellow's first name was Magnus, and he asked Darby to go into business with him in a house building company, jointly owned by Magnus and Darby.

The company was duly set up as agreed, Darby was to be the project manager, Magnus would be the general manager, and responsible for the administration of the office. Each partner was to put up the capital amount as agreed and each would co-guarantee the bank loans. Because of his military service Darby had no trouble to raise the money, he needed and to give the guarantee. Murray, Darby's brother, agreed to work for the new company and would be the foreman.

The first contract was with the New Zealand Government, and was for the construction of twenty homes. The business started off quickly and was very successful, quite quickly the company was completing from start to finish ten houses per week and growing. Most of the workers were ex soldiers and all were very keen to see the company doing well.

Murray proved to be a very hard worker and a good leader, although his constant boasting was a small problem for some of the men. Magnus and the team all got on well; he was fondly called old Mag; but it was all in fun and very respectful. Darby and Magnus were obviously very compatible, each one stuck to his own work with great mutual effort. Magnus Constructions Ltd soon began to earn a very good reputation, with the Government Housing Department; and was given as much work as they could handle, and whatever contracts they wanted. For the first five years, they were content to build the business to a sound position, and then they moved to doing private homes, and eventually building homes with company funds and selling them. (Spec building).

In those days all construction was done on site, there was no such thing as pre- assembled doors and frames, or trusses etc. Concrete was all mixed on site and there were teams for the various sections of work, ie the concrete team, framing and roof joists, internal and external walls, flooring and finishing. It was all split up so that each team had approximately the same amount of work on each section. Magnus constructions were quite advanced; they were the first ones to set up a factory to bulk produce joinery which included windows, doors, and roof trim frames; this they did very successfully. Next they moved on and started doing frames and roof trusses all preassembled for onsite finishing. Finally they started to buy pre mixed concrete delivered by trucks which mixed the concrete as they travelled to the building sites.

Very soon, "on site they had been doing everything" they now did almost 50% in their factory or bought in ready to assemble. Magnus constructions were really moving along very quickly, when all of a sudden old Mag died what a catastrophe! Could the company carry on? Old Mag had been the brains of the outfit and Darby had been glad to leave all that controlling work to Mag, now he was gone. Darby and Murray got together and decided to close Magnus Constructions and form Stephens Contractors, but they decided they would do mainly industrial work, building large factories, which was more profitable.

The owners would be Darby and Murray jointly, now Darby would do old Mags job, and Murray would be the project manager. Once again they were very successful, but they no longer needed to make joinery or frames and trusses so that factory was sold. Old Mags widow was paid out a fair price for her husband's share of the business 50% of what it was sold for, and the new company started out debt free.

Meanwhile Darby had been married to his former housekeeper and had a daughter by her, Leanne named after her mother, quite an attractive child but the new wife and their child, was never able to get on with Darby's and Dawn's children. Darby's first family saw the new wife as just a gold digger, who had snagged a successful businessman.

Darby had tried to foster Winty (his nephew) when he had come out of the army; he believed that the potential was there for him to take over the company when he and Murray retired. Darby's sons had showed they were not interested and did not have the ability anyhow, in the family only Winty had the intelligence; and the personal drive to push the company on and Darby knew that well. Darby tried hard to get Winty to settle down and work for the family, but it was a lost cause Winty would listen to nobody, and after his Grandmother (me) died, there was no way he would be staying in Auckland. Winty had been away for a long time, so Darby decided he was going down to Christchurch by himself to visit which turned out to be a great trip. Winty was so pleased to see his uncle; and the two of them got on famously just as they had in years gone by. Darby was not happy; he was mourning his ruined marriage, but he did not tell Winty. After staying for seven days, and having reassured himself that his nephew was well and doing fine, Darby went home and tried to console himself.

Winty had decided to set up a branch of his business in Auckland and Darby helped him to get established. The new branch was a huge success at first, but because of problems that were unfortunate and abnormal the company, after such an impressive start failed. Darby was very sad at the failure but could not help Winty, because the problems created were way too many, and too large.

Darby and Murray went on to run their business, but the first shock was the death of Robert, Darby's youngest child, a son. Robert had done his apprenticeship with Stephens's constructions and was a qualified carpenter, but he was recognized as a smooth speaking con man. Having conned somebody out of a small sum of money, Robert got beaten up; we never knew by whom; he died of his injuries.

Robert had been quite a handsome and personable young man, but the family was all aware he was developing into a real con man, he had been accused on several occasions but been saved by his Fathers position. His mother Dawn had been really heartbroken, that her youngest child was going haywire in the extreme. Unlike Andrew he had never been fond of sport nor had he ever been close to his parent's.

Darby had not even recovered from that disaster when Andrew the Eldest child died, addicted to liquor as his Father had been before him he died of a heart attack, he was at the time of his death only 35 Years of age, and over 180 kilograms in weight. I felt sad that I had not been able to help Andrew, by the time I arrived it was too late, .Andrew had loved his Dad so much and had gone haywire when his other went off and married a fellow, he knew and never liked. Andrew accused his mother of being plain stupid, it was from then he went on a beer drinking binge, from which he never stopped. In truth he deliberately drank himself to death!

There was so much sadness around! I could see and sense that in my grand-daughter Cheryl; born to Dawn and Darby. The death of her mother and then her only brothers had been devastating! Cheryl as daughters often do idolized her Dad and accused her mother of killing him, even though her mother had died before Darby. Cheryl took some time to recover from the loss of her family, two brothers' and her Mum and Dad. She eventually married and had two children but she is still bitter towards her mother.

It was also sad for me to observe that Leanne, born to Darby and his ex-housekeeper, now wife, and Cheryl had never got on. Leanne was named after her Mother who came to Darby's home when she applied for a house keeper's job that Darby had advertised. She became pregnant within 3 months to Darby and he married her immediately. None of the family ever accepted Darby's new wife Leanne, which may have been the reason she never settled into their marriage. Anne accused Leanne of just being a gold digger who had enticed Darby to her bed, to be fair that would not be very hard to have done. It would have made a world of difference, if the half sister could have been there for each, other at such trying times.

Due to my continued work on Darby, I can happily say that I witnessed an enormous change coming over his life; he had stopped his womanizing, heavy smoking and drinking, even through all of his sadness, he never broke out again of that I was very grateful. Every now and again he would go on a binge and I would have to start all over again, just trying to get him back to where he was before the slipped up. He was treating his children better than before so that was one blessing, but oh, how he missed Dawn! It was so sad to watch him pining after what he could never again have; his one and only sweet heart.

Darby and Murray were both now aging and had no family to take over the company. Darby's sons were both dead and neither had had the ability to run the company anyhow. Murray's son was not interested; there were only girls left neither of whom; had ever been involved in business. Darby's health was starting to fail; years of smoking and drinking had given him liver, kidney and heart problems, there seemed little hope he would live much longer. For a while he carried on running the business, and finishing up contracts the company had committed to. The old staff where now gone mostly retired and doing nothing. The young staff had no interest in Stephens Contractors; to them it was just another job, so there was little point to keep the company going.

The last contract the company did was to build the new abattoirs out at Westfield, when that was finished the plant was sold up and the company was closed down with all responsibilities met. Darby had a very nice home in Meola Rd Pt Chevalier. After selling his home, left his second wife Leanne, and his two daughters, Cheryl and Leanne the proceeds of everything he had.

Darby was told he had no choice but to have an operation, for his many health problems and that it should be as soon as possible. He was told by the doctors there was a good chance he would not survive the operation, but if they did not try he would certainly die. He never came out of the operation, and passed away peacefully. I was there to greet Darby when he arrived in heaven and to my great relief he was accepted into the inner family of spirits, he was so happy to see me and for me it was a triumph, I had saved one of my children from Satan. Darby chose after a period to be rebirthed, he selected a family of course we did not know where our loved ones chose to go, they were happy that's all that mattered.

Chapter 4

Murray:

I had thought things will be better with Murray and I was right. Yes it was better in the way that there was no booze or womanizing but, the pride and arrogance along with his cigarette smoking, almost suffocated all those around him. The first day, Murray was busy telling his son and daughter just how clever he was. That he could outwork any two men together, and he could do any carpentering job better than anybody else in the firm.

If it was not for me he said, Darby would go broke, he does not even realize just how much I do to keep the company going. Yes dad! The two kids agreed they had obviously heard this tirade so many times it was boring. Nothing would stop Murray, he wanted everybody to know just how superior he was, not only did he tell Darby, but everybody else in the firm as well.

Murray was my second youngest; four years older than Claire, he was the darkest of my children, but like me he had very European features. He was the most difficult in that he always wanted to be alone, and had a habit of going off on his own to my own, and his father's distress. Murray was very good at sports and excelled at rugby. Like most of my children he was good at school, but since it was only a small country school, perhaps the education may have been a little below national standards.

When Arthur passed away Murray became a loner, and seemed to become withdrawn. When war broke out in Europe, Murray was just seventeen years of age and announced he was going to enlist in the Maori battalion, with his brothers. My objections were loud and strenuous, but ignored, when he came home with documents to sign, his attitude was such that in spite of my fears I signed.

When he had come home from the war Murray had been really wild, he was not like Darby, he just would not be controlled, whenever he went out there was sleepless nights for me. He was such a boastful fellow, and always looking for a fight! There was a hotel not far away from where he was living, and so many nights we were called out to take him home, he was just passed out from drinking wine, and had been in some fight.

I was at my wits end and didn't know what to do, he would wake up in the morning and always go to work, but when he did not get home in the evening, it would totally spoil the rest of my day. One episode was when we were called; and Murray was like a caged tiger, shouting abuse at everyone and even after he saw me did not stop. The owner of the hotel was losing patience, because as he told me Murray was chasing good customers away, with his crazy carry on almost every day after working hours. Murray had been told he was not wanted in the hotel, but he refused to listen and kept coming anyhow. This night in particular he had attacked two men, both of whom were normally his friends, but now were just wanting to fight Murray because they had been so abused they were sick of him, and would take no more.

I tried to get Murray to leave but he would not even listen to me, it was impossible. All of a sudden there was a total brawl with Murray in the middle. To my horror I had to watch one of my sons get himself beaten up by three men who attacked him all at once, it must be said that he gave as good as he got, but it's not for a mother to see such a drunken mess.

When he met Alma it all changed he stopped drinking and fighting immediately. They lived together for twelve months, the night Murray proposed Alma came with him to see me and she was so excited, in my case since it seemed obvious they would marry; all I thought was; it's about time!

On that morning after I had arrived to watch over them, Alma his wife came in and asked are you going to take the kids to Sport dear? I have a busy time this morning! Oh sure said Murray I would love to take them, what's on today? Let's go, come on where are we are going I bet I can beat the both of you. Yeah dad they said, we know you always tell us that and it's always the same; you tell everybody how good you are, and how at our age you were so much better than us; we don't really want to go, to be honest. Murray's demons were not so many, but they were still looking pretty pleased with themselves. I was thinking…Gee… I sure have a big job to do! I wander how the girls are getting on

Murray was always at his boastful best after work in the evenings. Alma obviously idolized him and just agreed with anything he said, she just took it all in with a grain of salt and a smile, encouraging him to think more of practical things. Murray was the grand orator; he told all who would listen and a lot who would not, just why he was so superior to his brother, and why he was the vital cog in the company. He even told Darby just how lucky he was, to have a brother like him save his business. Darby took it all in with a smile, and agreed that Murray was totally indispensable, so long as Murray was happy; Darby was happy so why did it matter?

With Murray I could remember nothing that had set him to feeling that he was superior, so I had to look for why he was really feeling so inferior, there could be no other reasoning. There had been nothing in our home in any way that would create the problem. Murray had only been 17 when he signed up to go to war, and he had no previous challenges of a physical nature, he was the youngest boy and he had always been catered to by the two older brothers and his father, so I had no memory bank to go too.

Murray had been but a boy when he signed up for the Maori Battalion, and he had left New Zealand before he turned eighteen, so I had little to go on. I thought back of when they had left and when they had returned, and could find little by way of clues. When he was in the military camp he had started to get a little difficult, but his brother Dick was there and could always control both of his brothers, but the start of a difficult temperament, was starting to show. Murray had returned as a total rebel, his main occupation when first released from the forces was drinking and fighting; it seemed he lived to fight nobody could make it out.

Then when he started drinking wine it was really a big problem, he just went berserk when loaded up with wine, if they could keep him on the beer he was controllable. When Murray arrived back, he was only 23, so it was very difficult to work out just what had happened, he would take no caution from anyone but then he met Alma, and it all changed. Murray gave up drinking alcohol and womanizing; he lived for only one person, Alma. We had all heaved a sigh of relief! They settled down and married within a short period of time so the problem was not there anymore. The only one other thing I could think of that would have affected his life in such a very devastating way, was the war he had taken part in.

In searching back through Murray's background I found that he had been a prisoner of war for four years. Whatever it was that had had such a tremendous impact in his young life, had to have been within that period. I also found that like Darby, Murray had spent time in the Vatican or Rome after the War, on his way home. So I had a suspicion that once again things had gone terribly wrong, and if I was going to help him deal with his demons, I would have to dig deeper; but how was I to find out what the problem was?

The first thing I did was go back through the records of Murray's church and political activities, and I found a strong political interest so that was a clue. His church background had been the same as for all of us so I saw little problem there, but who knows there was nothing in Darby's background either. Then after a great deal of difficulty, I was able to trace back some of the background relating to Murray's imprisonment, and I found out he had spent most of the time with men far older than him with strong political views; so he had been indoctrinated in many different ways. Murray was after all just a boy who had no general knowledge whatsoever, these men would have been mentors to a youth; just a boy soaking up anything and everything around him.

Murray had like Darby finished up in Rome on his way home but he had far more extravagant views of the Vatican War activities. Murray was convinced that Pope Pius VI was an apologist for the Germans. Pius VI was reputed to have not taken any positive action at any time, towards sending out a call for Catholics to support the Jews in their time of real need, he had not called for support of any kind even though he was well aware of the atrocities being committed. Worse, Pius VI was actually seen as a Hitler sympathizer, by the men Murray was with, so he did indeed have very firm views on the Catholic Church, and of those calling themselves representatives of God on earth.

It also became obvious that Murray felt inferior because he had virtually sat the War out in a Prisoner of War Camp, which is why on coming home he actually manifested an inferiority complex, so at last the truth was coming out. Well the truth will set us free, but how was I to bring Murray and his family truth; this was going to be a lot harder than Darby. I had to spend a lot of time to think this one out!

The other big problem I could see Murray had was his chain smoking, he always had a lit cigarette in his mouth. That also was going to be a hard habit to crack, the abuse of his body in this way; was obvious from his severe smokers cough. To me Murray's problem seemed a lot more difficult to deal with than Darby's. I was so glad he was the last of the boys, except Winty, (My eldest Grandson) from whom I was sure there would be no problems.

I looked forward to the girls I thought for sure they would be a lot easier, but I had to get to them first. I could see a long time before I would be able to see some success with Darby and Murray, but at least I was becoming experienced in my new job, and started to have a feel for what I was doing.

I just thanked our Lord and Savior day and night for the superiority of our forces, it was so obvious that we were outnumbered by at least 10 to 1, but our Spiritual superiority was becoming to me ever increasingly obvious. The numbers did not matter it was the strength of our Spiritual convictions, and the reality of love against hate that was so obvious. The great amount of noise that Satan's demons kicked up was totally out of place, we were the achievers they were the screamers, and I could now see it so clearly. I was beginning to really enjoy my work, because it was so obvious what was happening.

I had begun to notice how much people had changed from when I was young, and my family was growing up. We Stephens had all thought and worked together as a unit, if somebody outside our family group needed help we gave it gladly, but now there was no such thing as giving help. Everybody was in a big hurry there was no time to relax no time for anything, time was the most valuable commodity of all and you gave it away to nobody. Even your own family had no time, it was a terrible reality that was coming through to my understanding, and I was just amazed. Mother and Father rarely met they were always moving through to another engagement, so long as the kids looked after themselves that was fine, occasionally they could get together on the weekends if they were lucky.

It was so with Murray and Alma both were very busy, Alma did dressmaking and Murray of course as he told everybody ran controlled, and was the back bone of Stephens Contractors. Murray left home at 600 am and arrived home at 1900 pm; Alma left at 800 am and arrived home at 1600pm. Their children, Brian & Judith, were good kids, but were not getting the Parental supervision, they should have had. Both children tried hard to avoid their Father, but idolized their Mother; she tried hard to make up to them for their Fathers constant boasting.

So the problem was how was I to get through to Murray? Was it to be the same method as Darby? Somehow I knew Murray would be far harder to crack than Darby, to me only Alma had the influence to get through to him, but she seemed quite happy with her lot; so how was I to proceed. The children were definitely not happy, but I could not see how they could exert any influence on their Father, no! It had to be Alma. Only she had ever had any real influence over him, the opening gambit had to be the cigarettes; she could quite easily be influential about the drastic problems with smoking. I had to inculcate her in that area first, but I did not see that as all that hard. I started immediately awakening Alma's conscience towards the dangers of smoking, and she came out very quickly and put the pressure on Murray.

Murray of course resisted but Alma was persistent and the more she learned through her dreams about the dangers of smoking, the more persistent she became, it was a classical case of Mother knows best, the more Murray resisted the more she insisted. I watched in fascination who was going to win Husband or Wife, I kept the pressure up and made sure that Alma kept dreaming of smoke related illnesses, and the more she did the more she got stuck into Murray. I was delighted as I saw a steady decrease in the smoking until finally there were no more. The cigarettes smoking had ceased. Now the real problems began. How was I going to get through to him about his personal boasting and pride? I had to do something urgently to stop the alienation that was slowly being created between father and children due to his persona. It was going to have to be a different and complete change, of that I was sure!

After praying for guidance from our Father in heaven, I began to feel the power of his wisdom start to flow through me, it was incredible. The first thing to do was to interest Murray in politics again and all that took was some memories from the past, in the form of pleasant dreams that was meant to stop him from obsessing about work. This would mean he would start to acquire outside interests, but once having done that I had to steer things around to the past, to get him released from whatever had been the obsession, from which he had had to be released, and that was not going to be so easy.

Murray responded easily to suggestions of political interest; the enthusiasm was there and it was strong, but how to keep it in control. His wartime memories came flooding back quite unprovoked by me, the problem was one of control, not to let it get out of hand and create a nightmare. All of a sudden Murray began to talk about his memories and his dislike of the Catholic Church; this was not what I was after I did not want to create theological argument just the opposite. I wanted to wipe out the unpleasant past, and replace it with a truth of how important a real walk with Christ would be.

I began to feel as if I was treading on a fine line and I prayed, lord help me to control what I am unleashing, give me the wisdom I need, to guide my son into a beautiful truth, not an ugly world in which he was retreating from truth, and hiding in a world of ugliness. It was going to be a very sensitive path, to be treading, and I could see it was necessary to be very sensitive so as to play my part properly. The important part (I thought) was to enthuse Alma; but how?

Alma had no memories I could restore to her, she simply responded to Murray's reactions, she just wanted him to be happy, but she recognized the need of her children so in a way she was a conduit but a rather vague one. Alma had always wanted to keep Murray happy she seemed to think Murray might change his mind and leave her yet I never did see any reason for her to feel that way.

From the day Murray met Alma he had changed. Alma was a full sister to Owen, Anne's husband and I think she was a little ashamed of Owen. She had three other brothers and all were a little like Owen.

I had to very carefully select good memories for Murray of when he was a boy dependant on his Father and brothers. I tried to restore his self confidence in a genuine sense, not warped ideas fed into him by fellow Prisoners of War; with time to waste and no real sense of direction.

More importantly I tried to bring him positive thoughts about the modern day Catholic Church, it was important that his memories of such extremism be removed and replaced with real and positive thoughts, but that for me was far from easy. The Catholic Church has always been a very positive feature of the New Zealand way of life, their participation in so many areas of the community is well documented. I had to bring this gently to Murray's notice, being always careful to avoid any mention of the hierarchical central structure, and to certainly avoid anything to do with the Vatican and its leadership that would be a disaster.

It was difficult for me to be all the time arguing for the Catholics when we had been Protestants but because we knew that heaven was none denominational it did not really matter. Sometimes though it still seemed strange that the world was so full of Catholics, and it was hard not to agree that the enormous wealth they had accrued seemed to be an abomination. When the boys spoke with such anger about the riches they had seen in the Vatican we wandered just what could be done if anything

It was not so much resorting to the past but to highlight what was going on now, and to avoid all mention of the past so I concentrated on making sure his everyday memories were sharp, and clear about all Catholic activities. I was very careful however to provoke memories of all sorts of other activities, that would provoke Murray's mind in a positive way, anything and everything that would start to create real self confidence, not based on false memories, but based on what was happening around him and how he could be a part of all that activity.

It was very hard because at the same time I had to teach Alma to be more assertive with her husband for her children sake; it was a sensitive path, it began to take shape very slowly, but still it was happening. I had to get the children to appreciate the difference in their dad as he began to move into new areas, ones of which the whole family could be proud, not just a continual diet of Murray's self assertion. It was hard because I had to get Murray to lead out first, and to get him to leave his area of comfort which was not easy.

Murray had become so self-absorbed in self-praise, that he had almost forgotten how to be simply truthful to himself, that was a slow painful process and having only memories and present day events to work with, I was a very slow and painful process. Alma's support was crucial, as ever she supported any little thing Murray said or did, so in a way she was not so effective, but the children were; they were so enthusiastic about anything that stopped their Father talking about himself, they just did everything possible to discourage him and it was beginning to work, slowly but surely Murray was starting to change.

Murray began to take a strong interest in Public Affairs and he eased-up talking about himself so much, but he still could not slow down when it came to work; he just wanted to maintain his aggressive position with the company; instead of having less work time, he was now more committed and struggling to keep up. But he was becoming far more open minded about the church in every day affairs.

Murray still could not tolerate that the church should have a say in public life; he was very firm on that, yet began to accept the primacy of church in certain activities (i.e.) charity at home and abroad, certain tax exemptions for building programs etc, business tax exemptions for church trading trusts.

His opposition to the Catholic Church however grew stronger, it was as if he would never forget his time in the Vatican and he spoke out frequently against what he termed "that man at the top", it was an obsession and as such it had to be broken, he could not be free until he could relieve himself from these memories from his past.

I believed I was making headway. Began to like my job; it all seemed so worthwhile to see the ones I love, slowly but surely being released from Satan's icy grip and the demons were slowly becoming far quieter and less arrogant I should not had commenced to congratulate myself too quickly because Murray suddenly got himself elected to a position as a keynote speaker for his local RSL, (Returned Services League) the subject was to be the view of a returned soldier, having seen the ravages of what War had done to the local populace especially in Italy.

I sensed trouble straight away, but I knew there was nothing I could do; it took time to reprogram a mistake, and I did not have time. Murray started off ok and I thought well, no trouble so far this is going to be fine, if only he kept off from Politics. Murray described how he had seen the effect on the local Italian population, he stressed that the shame was that it was a war for which the Romans had no heart; they were not behind Hitler in the first place.

The Italian's Murray declared had been seduced by their leader Mussolini who had in fact as a fascist, merely tried to copy the apparent glory of Hitler, and had led his people into a war they had no heart for. I began to think ok, so that's what he learnt in the POW camp, I hope he does not start to get radical here and blow up all of his -so far- good work. This is precisely what Murray proceeded to do he entered the theological debate with great gusto, and before I knew it his previously well received speech was in tatters.

Murray let out a torrent of unrehearsed abuse against Pope Pius VI and he gave it with the entire trimmings, Nazi sympathizer etc. oh my! I could see the delight on the faces of his Demons; they were ecstatic and dancing around screaming with delight; I on the other hand realized we had made a mess which we would have to move to fix as best we could and sooner better than later. The following day the Newspapers ran the headlines "RSL leader" attacks the Pope, and all the usual tabloid stuff. Murray was not an RSL leader; he was simply a returned soldier with anti Catholic views.

That's not how his speech was reported! In no way was he a leader and he had made his views known to the RSL; the media chased him to see whether he was interested in saying anything else. He became an overnight sensation and he loved it! From the point of view of someone simply stating a position there was no great drama, as a leader which he was not! He had simply been elevated by the sensationalism of the media!

Murray had become real news on print and TV to headline value. So instead of bringing Murray under control I had let a Tiger out of its cage, Murray now had a national soap box, he was not about to sit down and shut up there was no way. I realized it was but a short term sensation and he would soon be forgotten, but the only one that did not know that was Murray; he was now worse than ever. Somehow I had to try to bring him slowly back to where he had been heading towards, and I had to do it gently but quickly.

The situation demanded urgent action and I moved towards it as quickly as I could without doing further damage, it was a case of returning to some not so pleasant War memories, and there were plenty of those, but we could not overdo it otherwise it could turn into one more negative episode. I revived some of the memories from Murray's POW day's camp, being with some of his mentors knowing full well that as an adult he would not be as impressionable, as he was as a boy. Some of those memories were accurate for 1945, but certainly inappropriate for now. I could see that Murray was becoming less than enthusiastic day by day, as the old memories flooded back, not only because of my help; Murray realized he had made a mistake, and he had done it on a national basis, so how was he to make amends to the RSL and the Catholic Church.

It was a good example of the Lords guidance, I had started the whole thing rolling, but had been monitored and it was really under control. While Murray was still newsworthy, he came out and admitted his views had been learned in a POW camp as a teenager, and he had spoken out foolishly. He apologized to both the RSL and the Catholic Church, and reiterated they were views he had learned as a young prisoner, and he was as devastated as any one when he had the chance to listen to his own foolish tirade. We got the Lords blessing all right because the whole thing died down as quickly as it flared up, and we were back to where we were making good progress.

The great thing about the whole episode was the obsession Murray had previously held against the Catholics was all gone, he had no more thoughts for or against them, and he very quickly forgot the whole episode. A goal had been reached quite naturally and really I was delighted. I had got a shock when the whole thing started, but it had all come together to me for good in my love of Our Lord Jesus. To resume we had achieved a lot but not enough. I had to help him get over the inferiority complex he had displayed; I started my new task with great vigor, since I knew we had got rid of a major hurdle. I commenced by refreshing Murray's youth memories once again, through his dreams.

There were memories from before the POW camp and we started to remind him of who he was and how he was before he went to War; it seemed to be just the treatment he needed he visibly changed. It was as if a great load had been lifted from his shoulders, gone was the need to be the best and the strongest etc.

Back for a quick check on Darby; he was progressing nicely and improving steadily on his diet of positive dreams. It was becoming truly heartening both of my sons seemed to be progressing, but there was still a great load of work to be done before the end-result could become visible to the naked eye, and that was a commitment to be in Gods Spiritual Army.

Murray was a tremendous worker, but he tended to take a lot of risks. One day while they were doing an industrial contract there was a big trench to be dug, I could not believe what I was seeing; the drainage team had refused to go down into an enormous trench for fear the sides may collapse, and they would be buried. They were discussing just how they were going to shore up the sides of the trench, and just how much they were going to charge the company for the extra work.

Murray came up and asked what the hold-up was? But when it was explained to him he let out an exclamation of anger and jumped in the trench himself, and completed the job without shoring up the sides. Then he jumped out of the trench and sacked the two men, who had wanted the shoring done for extra money. I still don't know if he was being fair or not, but it looked dangerous to me at that time. Another time he came along and asked why some work had not been completed, when told the job was too dangerous, Murray promptly did the job himself and sacked the men who had opposed his views. At this time he had toned down his boasting, but perhaps his actions in some ways were worse than his boasting, certainly for his staff it was worse.

Murray had been granted a rehab government home as a returned soldier, so he had never built one for himself, he had no need. He bought the one the Govt gave him cheap and dreamed of the day he would retire and build a home to retire to, but that would not be until he was ready. Alma was very happy with the idea, so they never spent money on their home over the years, just lived on there quite happily. Murray's chain smoking had undermined his lungs; and he developed cancer even though he had stopped, sadly we had been too late, and there was nothing that could be done. To his credit Murray did not start smoking again as so many do when faced with cancer. Alma of course was devastated, but buckled down and encouraged him to continue on with building their retirement home.

Their daughter Judith was a tall girl over six feet high and solid, not fat, she had qualified as a school teacher and was apparently a very good and popular teacher. Sadly she died very young only 35 YOA from heart problems, it was a disaster to Murray and Alma this on top of the cancer Murray had contracted was hard for them to take. Judith had been very good at school and had won several awards and a scholarship to one of the top schools in Auckland, but she had always been aware of her height. To make that worse, she was also sensitive to Murray's boasting and seemed to cringe whenever he started one of his tirades. Brian their Son was a very quiet fellow as a child and grew up to be the same as a man; brother and sister were very close, Brian also was not happy to hear one of Murray's outbursts.

Brian was a qualified builder, he had done his apprenticeship with the family company, and like his father, and he was a top tradesman and a great worker. When his Father was diagnosed with cancer and his sister died, Brian almost gave up; he was single and had no responsibilities and, did not see much point in it all, he was thirty years of age with no steady girl-friend. After Brian had mourned for his Sister and the health of his Father for twelve months, but he pulled himself together and told his father he was going to go and help finish the new home, so his parents could move in quickly. The idea he told his parents was to have his father retire, and see his parents spend their last years in retired comfort.

Murray and Alma for their part agreed to put their current house on the market, and as soon as it was sold Murray would stop work as would Alma, and they would do as Brian suggested and move into their new house even if it was not fully finished. Murray and Darby had already agreed to sell up the business, sell everything so there was nothing to do except finish any work there was left.

The new house was over 150 kilometers away from Auckland City, looking out over a beach in a beautiful position. As he promised, Brian quit his job and moved up to a small Bach close by in which he could live while he worked on the house. Murray had some small jobs left to do which he completed, then he was ready to go. Alma was going to stay in the house until it was sold, and then she was going to close it down until settlement. The old house was sold after three months, and Alma moved out and joined Brian and Murray, to help as much as she could to finish the new home.

The house was at the stage of lock up which means the roof was on windows and doors installed. (So we had heard father and son commenting). The electrical and plumbing fittings were in place, ready to be finished after the walls and floors were completed. The inner walls had the contractors working on them, and the floors were being laid. All this work only took a week to complete, and then the inner cupboards were installed, as well as kitchen and toilets.

It was great to see father and son work so close together! It really warmed my heart and I wished circumstances could have been different. Because of

Murray's cancer and short life expectancy, Brian had decided to shift into the house with his parents'; he wanted to be with his mother when the time came. After they had safely moved into the new home Murray's health seemed to rally, and with Alma they spent time just relaxing in each other's company, something they had never found easy to do, due to their previous heavy workloads.

Brian at this time gave his parents a pleasant surprise and introduced a girl to them, the first one he had ever shown himself to be really interested in. There had been no indication of what Brian was doing, but it was obvious the young couple were really smitten with each other. Within two weeks Brian announced they were getting married almost immediately, and preparations were almost complete. The wedding was small with a crowd of about fifty guests, mostly from Brian's family and it was very nice. Both of Brian's parents were very happy for the young couple!

Brian and his new wife left for a two week honeymoon, and one month after they returned Brian announced his wife was pregnant due in eight months. The baby was a boy and the first and only grandchild at that time, named after Murray. The baby was only three months old when another pregnancy was announced, this time it was a girl and named Wright Stephens after its Grandmothers maiden name.

Murray had recovered enough to enjoy the wedding and the two babies', but went into a rapid decline soon after. The doctors confirmed the family's fears that the end was near, no more than three months to live, was predicted. Alma's health now started to go bad and it was obvious she would not outlive Murray by very long; she seemed to have lost the will to live.

Murray died after two months and he must have been glad, for there was so much pain and discomfort in his final days. Alma died only thirty day after Murray, she died with a gentle smile on her face.

I was of course there to welcome Murray into heaven, it was an anxious time, but again it was a victory, my Son had been saved and it was another victory for Christ. Murray the same as Darby chose to be rebirthed.

Chapter 5

Anne Wright nee Stephens.

It was time now time to see how I could help Anne. At least I hoped she would be in a better condition and she was! Anne herself was in good condition, but her husband was not so great, he had been involved in an extra marital affair going on for several years.

Owens demons were many and varied; gambling, adultery. He was a man saturated with demons everywhere every bit as bad as Darby and every bit as sad. Annie had always been barren and her life had been an unhappy one, since she loved kids, but it was not to be she could not conceive. Owen had used everything possible to make Annie feel guilty, and he had a son of his own born from his adulterous affair of many years standing. I realized I was going to have to learn and know far more of my unhappy daughter's life, in the years ahead as I surveyed the task that had to be done.

Anne had been the third to last of my children, and had been considered the most intelligent, although we were blessed in that all except Winnie; would have been considered well above average. Anne had been a happy girl, always cheerful and ready to help anyone if she could, perhaps the one in the family most like her Father Arthur.

Anne and Claire had been very close, which since they were the two youngest girls was probably quite natural. There always seemed to be nothing Anne could not do, dressmaking a fabulous knitter, good cook, but a bit of a tomboy. She always wanted to compete with her brothers, since only Murray was in her age bracket; he was the one who was constantly harassed by Anne. Anne was also very good at school learning seemed to be very easy for her, Arthur believed she was going to be the brains of the family.

Dick who was the second eldest was very good at school too, but he was killed in WWII so we never knew what he could have achieved.

When Anne was sixteen her sister Millie who was by then married to Percy Browne, a White man in Auckland, suggested that Anne should come to live with her and Percy at Avondale. From there she was to be enrolled to attend Mt Albert Grammar school, and get a better education than she could get in North Auckland, there was no college of that caliber anywhere in the north. After discussing the matter between ourselves, Arthur and Me, and then with Anne decided to allow her to go and do as Millie had suggested. Had we known what was going to happen we would not have allowed her to go, but it was too late when we found out what had happened? Millie's Mother in Law we found out later hated Maori's and especially she hated that her Son had married one.

When Anne arrived she was enrolled at the college that part was fine, but she had to make certain she did not allow herself to be seen around the Browne house, and that she was living on the premises. Every night she had to wait until after dark to sneak in and climb up into the ceiling, into which a bed had been set up. Millie would save her scraps of food from the kitchen, and sneak that up for Anne's place in the ceiling for her meal. Then if she needed to go to the toilet she had to wait until after dark, and Percy's Mother had gone to bed, before she could come down to go to the toilet. Percy's Mother had been widowed during WWI and the Browne's were considered to be upper middle class at the time. For the rest of her life she never recovered from the shock of her son marrying a Maori! On the weekend when there was no school to attend, Anne was stuck in the ceiling until Monday, before it got light again. My poor daughter never let on to us under what terrible conditions she was living, but she never for the rest of her life forgave Percy Browne, for having put her through two years, of such a dismal home. By the time we came to live in Auckland, Anne had found casual work and had a little home of her own.

When the boys were in military camp they came home to where we were living in Freeman's Bay one week end, and had with them a fellow soldier who was in camp with them Mac McDonald. Anne was visiting and a romance started between her and McDonald; which resulted in marriage when he came home from the war with my two sons. Mac as we called him was like my children half caste Maori, and went to the war with the Maori battalion.

The marriage was a sad failure, Anne's inability to conceive was a problem for Mac so they parted after three years; and this was a shame. After her marriage failed, Anne met and married Owen Wright, who was a member of a large family, the Wrights. Their Mother was a full blooded Jamaican, and their Father was full blooded White. The progeny of that marriage four girls and four boys, were all extremely attractive, the males being very masculine, and the females very feminine.

After her second marriage Anne, started to smoke, and she did so for the rest of her life, until she died of emphysema at the age of seventy. Anne was unable to have children, and spent her life lavishing her love on Claire's children.

She worked until she was over sixty years of age! Her marriage to Owen Wright survived for over forty years, but it was always considered that she chose to ignore what was happening, (His Adultery) because of her own barren situation and her inability to give Owen a child. We lived at my home which had been allocated to me by the Government, because of my son's war efforts and having had one killed. Anne, Owen and Me lived together for ten years. I had Winnie and Albert's first Son living with me from birth, unlike Millie and Percy they never asked for their son back. Arthur was a little backward and never took Winty's place in my heart! An offer to buy the house from the Government was received, the price of $10,000 at the time was a lot of money, but we did pay the deposit and make the purchase.

Anne had started work in a factory working for Alex Harvey Ltd; a public company listed on the Auckland stock exchange. This was a large can making business with several large factories in Auckland, and a total staff of several thousand. It did not surprise me when she was transferred to the office of one of the smaller factories, situated in Freeman's Bay. After about four years with that company, Anne was promoted to Private Secretary of the Managing Director, at that company's big plant at Mt Wellington in Auckland. Anne like the rest of the family spoiled Winty, and she frequently bought him clothes as well as going with him to school interviews etc.

Anne was most proud of Winty, and that was because of his obvious ability, to look after himself from such a young age. Of course with Anne, there was also the fact she too could understand the agonies; Winty would have gone through with Percy Browne. But she had no sympathy for Millie, who she always said was silly to put up with the nonsense; she received from Percy and his horrible family.

For her entire adult life Anne was very close to Clare and George Kipa, and their flock of children. There was nothing she would not do for her sister; Clare's children seemed to be a substitute for her own lack of a family. Owen on the other hand was a bad influence on that family!

Owen was an incurable gambler and he led Barry Kipa astray from the time Barry was very young, this was by encouraging him to follow Owens's gambling addiction. Anne and Owen often argued over his leading Barry astray, but it made no difference. Barry has had his life completely ruined by gambling, I know that can't all be blamed on Owen, but he was the one who first lit the light, but then also cultivated that unhealthy lust, in both of their lives.

Anne suffered from Gall Stones from the age of 45, and had to be hospitalized several times. The time she spent in hospital, created the opportunity for Owen to spend most of that time with his girlfriend. He rarely visited his wife in hospital, and seemed unaware of the acute pain associated with her health problem; sadly he made it obvious he did not really care.

Owen was spoilt by Anne who waited on him in every way day and night. Owen ate a very unhealthy, diet his special food was Steak and Eggs with Chips really lathered, all over with tomato sauce. Then he plastered the meal with butter, and his main condiment was toast, which was also heavily laid out with butter. This was his main meal on at least four nights per week, the other nights his food was equally unhealthy. Normally his lunch would be meat pies on work days, but about six eggs, bacon (or sausages) and toast all heavily layered with sauce and butter on the weekends. Breakfast was porridge and cream again with toast heavily buttered. Strangely he never got fat because his work was on his own milk round, so he was running every morning and during the day, when his run was finished he normally helped out one of his brothers, who was a bricklayer.

As Anne grew older she smoked more heavily, and spent far more time with Clare. When she retired at sixty years of age, Anne became very bored with having nothing to do. The same applied to Clare who now had all of her children grown up and off her hands. The two women got jobs as cleaners at Middlemore Hospital. Neither needed the money, but both needed something to do so figured, they may as well be paid for doing something. The two sisters used to have a great time going to work at the hospital, but all good things must come to an end and sadly their time did not last so long.

Owen went on his own selfish way and paid no attention to what Anne was doing, even though she always made certain he was being well looked after. Their home was always immaculately cleaned, and the garden which Owen did look after was always very nicely kept. They always had a good crop of vegetables growing and several fruit trees, the crops of fruit and vegetables they never ate, but gave away everything that grew to Clare or one of her family.

Owen never ate healthy food, and Anne never ate very much anyhow, her main sustenance seemed to be tea and toast, with a thin spread of jam and butter. Anne in her last days was suffering badly from emphysema, but she still drove herself almost daily to Clare's home, and the two would sit and smoke together. In spite of her health Anne would not give up her smokes, even though she knew death was very near. When Anne died in Middlemore Hospital she could only breathe with a terrible effort, it must have been a great relief for her to go. The two sisters shared their last moments together, and a big family funeral was held. Ironically after Anne died, in a very short time Owen also died, and he went still mourning for Anne. Anne was so happy to see me and of course for me it was great, I knew my three sons had been saved now only Winty, Winnie and Claire were still to be saved.

Anne decided she wanted to be rebirth in the hope of being blessed with plenty of children in her next life, we parted so happily.

Chapter 6

Claire.

So it was on to Claire and what a pleasure it was, after the dismal time I had spent with the other five children. Dick of course was dead and had never come back from the war. Clare was in Hospital and had been for several months, she had tuberculosis of the spine, and was in back braces and was not allowed to move, poor Claire! But she was cheerful and resigned to her fate, and her Family was a sight to behold, not many demons here and those that were certainly were not singing in triumph. It was amazing they had seven children all young and yet George nurtured them all. There was a steady routine in the house George got them ready for school etc; fed them and then left for work riding his push bike.

The older boys took control, and saw that everybody left for school properly. After work about 3.00 pm George came home and prepared the evening meal, which he then left for the boys to serve out when they all got home. Then George rode his push bike, 35 minutes to the hospital to see Claire, and then back home by about 9.30 pm. It was a daily ritual while Clare was in that brace in hospital for eight months. During all that time George only missed visiting his wife once and that was when the bike broke down. I am not saying it was a perfect household, but it was a very good one. There were a few demons around but they were well controlled, there was a lot of alcohol consumed, the boys sometimes gave their Dad a hard time.

There were a few cigarettes, but altogether a home that was totally saturated with family love. What a pleasure! After the first work I had done with my sons, this was going to be quite easy. Strangely enough, within the whole family there was no sign or any recognition of the Bible and the truth of Christ, it was a common thread through them all. No knowledge of Gods Kingdom!

Clare the youngest of my children had been a very placid and happy baby, and then grown into an easy natured child. When Winty was born there was a short period of natural jealousy, then she overcame that and took over as a little mother to her nephew. Winty for his part adored Clare, and was always looking for his Clarela, Where Clarela? He would wail if she was not around.

Clare was only nine years old when Winty was born so in many ways they grew up together, especially since Winty was so intelligent and quick to understand, from a very young age. Arthur spoiled the both of them outrageously, and always carried peanuts and sweets in his pockets for them. As soon as he arrived home from the shop both of those kids would be vying for first access to his pockets. Dick also spoiled them both, he loved his little sister so much, and he thought Winty was a toy for him to play with.

Whenever the family went out to the gum fields Clare's job was to mind Winty, and they played for hours on the sand dunes while the family worked. Gum digging was hard work, but because of the whole family involvement they all loved it, only Arthur never went out to the gum fields, he had his business to manage.

When it was decided we were going to shift to Auckland to be near my Sons, Clare was excited as any young girl would be, by that time she was nearly fifteen years of age, and wanting to go to the big city. Winnie had never been close to the others of my children or her siblings. I guess she could be considered as the odd one out, but she also was happy to be leaving Waihopo, and going to the big city.

When we had packed up everything and closed down the shop, sold all stock and given away what we could not sell, it was time to go. We travelled to Auckland by train and Clare endured that long slow trip like a fully grown adult. Winty slept most of the way, when he woke he was immediately a little nuisance. As soon as we arrived Claire was a great in helping me to get to our temporary home, but she like the rest of his was not happy at our temporary digs. Both girls went to stay with Anne the day after we arrived, which left Winty and me by ourselves for the first time.

Claire lived with Anne until we found a house in Freeman's Bay, then she moved back in with Winty and Me, and we were a happy little family. At seventeen years of age, Clare met George I never knew where, but I loved him from the start and thankfully Clare did to. The subject was never discussed, but I think both of them had never had any other relationship, it was wonderful to see how well they got along together from the start.

George was an unusual full blooded Maori, in that his dress and appearance was immaculate always, he smoked lightly and drank perhaps a little more alcohol than I would have liked, but he seemed to be unaffected by his drinking.

George never spoke bad language, and never missed work no matter what they had done; even a party that may have gone to the small hours of the morning, George would be up as sharp as ever and of to work. George had started work in the abattoirs as a slaughter-man in Thames at the age of twelve. By time he met Clare he was considered to be a top knife man! George was employed at Hellabys and stayed with that firm until he retired?

Claire was not a good housekeeper to start with, but like all of her sisters was a very good cook. She learned to be a good housekeeper though as her family grew so quickly, and she had a lot of work to do. Richard was born first and Grenville next, both very quickly and both were healthy babies. But it was her third son Walter that caused her so much heartache; he had serious skin eczema all over his body and especially his face. Claire used to bandage his little hands in desperation trying to stop him scratching, but to no avail his face was constantly bleeding, as he rubbed himself and cried because of the constant itch.

The next child Murray was also very bad with eczema, but he died before reaching his first birthday. While he was alive Clare was frantic trying to nurse the two of them, when little Murray was born Walter was only 18 months old and still scratching all the time.

Murray was worse than Walter and his itching was horrible to watch, the poor little fellow cried all of the time as he tried hard to scratch. Clare even tried to tie his little hands together but it was no use the little chap died and perhaps it was for the best, at least she saved one of the two. That tiny little coffin was so pitiful as it was taken away to the cemetery.

Until a house was allocated to me by the State I lived with Clare and George, but when the house came through it was time for us to split up. Winty was with Millie and Percy and since it was a three bedroom house the idea of shifting in by myself was silly, Anne and her first husband MacDonald shifted in with me and I took over care of Winnie's first child Arthur, named after his Grandfather.

Winty whenever he ran away from home always went to Clare, because she lived close to the centre of Auckland City and he knew how to get there. Winty never got to know where I now lived in the suburbs, until Clare's home was burned down, and then Winty came out to live with me. One of Clare's children had been playing with matches and set one of the beds alight, the whole house was burnt down very quickly, but luckily none of the children were hurt, Clare got them all out safely.

George's employers Hellaby's had provided the family with a home owned by the company. The house was a farm house land on which cattle owned by Hellaby's were left to graze until needed, but the farm house thankfully was vacant when the fire happened. George was considered by his employers as indispensable, and they proved their words when the need was there, they provided the family with a home. The family lived at that farm for over ten years until Clare and George bought a home of their own.

As his sons grew up George was a great example to his six sons and one daughter, his work ethic he passed on to his family, and he was very aware of his family's needs at all times. After Clare recovered from her tuberculosis of the spine she had two more sons which proved herself fully recovered, much to everyone's delight.

The Hellaby's farm was named browns farm, and we all delighted in going to visit them, it was a huge old house, but well kept and the children although they were not allowed to go out in the paddocks had lots of space to play. The three bedroom home they bought had a very large block of land, on which several fruit trees were planted. There was a large garage with a large room attached into which several beds were put, and since the family only had one girl there was lots of room for the boys who were still at home. That big room has been handy so many times for the Grandchildren to sleep in as well as visitors staying over.

George and Claire celebrated their fiftieth wedding Anniversary in 1992, and then their 60th in 2002 they have now been happily married for 66 years. The third son Walter who had suffered from eczema as a baby died from cardiac problems in 2004, he was seriously overweight. The Eldest Son Richard died in a swimming incident in 2005; both sad events were terrible blows to the old couple, and their siblings.

Only one daughter was born of Claire's marriage, Sonia she is the one who has been so attentive of her parents during their times of sickness. Sonia is married and has three children. The Kipa's have been and are a terrific family. Of the sons left, Grenville has now taken the position of the eldest. He was, the little fellow who was playing with matches and burned the house down in Freemans Bay. Then there is Barry; he is the one that did his meat apprenticeship with Winty's firm and is a top meat man. Unfortunately his marriage broke down because of his addiction to gambling. Denis is a panel beater and had some problem as we all do but his marriage is fine, both are fine men.

Steven is the youngest again with a fine marriage and a credit to his parents. George had been employed by Hellaby's from the time he and Clare married until he retired. He had been a top man for the company, but sadly Hellaby's collapsed and went into liquidation and all staff lost their jobs. George had been employed by that firm for almost forty years; they retired him with full recognition in spite of the collapse. George had reached the age for retirement anyhow so he became an old age pensioner.

Clare with her sister Anne took a job cleaning until she developed a none-malignant cancer. She went into hospital to have the cancer removed, like the time she had tuberculosis she fully recovered. George got cancer of the bowel for which he went into Middlemore Hospital and had a full recovery. At the same time Claire was in Middlemore for her general health problems, with both parents in hospital the family with grandchildren and great grandchildren gathered in mass to support the parents.

Sonia as usual was in the forefront of looking after her parents but she got help from her own daughters. Barry was staying with his parents also to keep an eye out for their welfare. Clare and George have had a great life together; they are so fondly loved by their family. Their life and family is as close in family Love as my family the Stephens had been, but of course our lives were changed by the WWII.

George and Clare recovered from their illness and returned home. They are now growing fragile from age, but George is happily looking after his wife with a very little help from Sonia. Apart from his own family the Kipa's are the love of Winty's life and always will be even though he is rarely there.

Chapter 7

―◦•◦•◦―

Millie.

My next visit was to my eldest daughter Millicent (Millie) and what a sorry sight she was, she had succumbed to her hard life and her mental health was in tatters. Millie had spent several years in a home for the mentally disabled and it was so sad. Her physical health always so robust was now but a shell, and she spent her days in solitude broken only, when her Daughters who loved her dearly, visited as often as they could. Her Sons and her husband were away farming and she saw little of them, so altogether she was a sad sight. The demons didn't consider people so disabled as a major threat, there was plenty of them around, but not in the numbers I would have expected, I left my eldest and then went to check out Winifred. (Winnie)

We had, had a great home but there were problems, in my own memories, the first to come to me was my temper always poorly controlled, and always ready to explode. My language was poor but in fact did not sound so bad since it was cloaked in half Maori half English, without much thought I could sheet home problems to myself. Now my beloved Arthur, he was never one to argue with me and he had left all decisions to me,

I was the head of the house. I had always planned and schemed to get my own way, and all major decisions were made by me. Arthur agreed with what I decided and if he did not I would kick up such a fuss he would withdraw and leave it all to me, so there it was the fruit of our own mismanaged family.

It was so strange wanting to get beside Millie who in fact spent her entire time in the past dreaming of when she was a girl, dreaming of having her children, but mainly dreaming of Percy her husband. In Millies eyes Percy could do no wrong, she lived in the good memories of him forgiving his adulterous activities. There appeared little for me to do, but I soon found this was wrong. Millie was a soul in torment and she lived in that state all of the time.

The memories that haunted Millie were as big as a legion. She was indeed a soul in pain. I almost wept as I began to get inside her head and to appreciate how one can suffer so much from Satan's Demons. They never let her rest. It was as if it were a perverse game always haunting Millie's memories; I realized here was a big job to be done. The demonic hordes in Millie's case were different in that they seemed a lot more sophisticated if that can be said about them. There was not the horrible cackling and laughing and triumphant sneers whenever they won a point, no this was totally different.

In Millie's case the demons were aggressive and physical they seemed to tear into her body and take perverse delight in digging into her shoulders with their talons, and enjoying the actual pain they inflicted. Of course the pain manifested in different ways, Millie would let out a sigh when attacked and it was horrible to watch, self immolation was one of the main attackers and it was her thoughts that laid the way open for the attacks. When this happened Millie would start to remember parts of her life that were destructive and the Demon would play out her thoughts.

The attacks on Millie became more destructive as her thoughts became more perverse. One day I realized she was remembering how one of her children, a daughter, had died as a four year old, the memories were so painful the demon was perched on her shoulder, and actually plunging its hands into her head, as a result it was as if she had a massive headache. Another was when she remembered trying to commit suicide, that demon constantly reminded her of the event; it was as if she could find no peace. Another was the memory of her husband's many infidelities; these demons haunted her all of the time, she could get no real peace until I could understand; how badly she was affected.

I knew that Jesus had cleansed out a legion of Demons from the man in the cemetery, but in my mind Millie seemed to have more than a legion of spirits and I was not Jesus. I knew I had to get them out; I wanted Millie to be cleansed and to stay clean. I knew that if she were able, Millie had a home she could go to especially with her eldest Daughter Aloma. I knew that was to be my goal; first to get her out and then to cleanse her of demons. The Demons considered me as a mortal enemy this was not like Darby and Murray. No not at all they were ready to fight!

This was to be, a direct confrontation and I was to be the aggressor, I did not like the idea, but I had to fight for my child so there it was the new challenge. Millie's day would start rather serene because she was so drugged up; she was beyond feelings, but as soon as the effect of the drugs began to wear off, the demons would be in a frenzy attacking her with everything, it was like they were having a feast. I often felt like attacking the demons as they tormented her, but I knew there was no way I could even contemplate that this was a spiritual war, and it had to be a spiritual victory.

Since the loss of her child was so painful and that demon so voracious, it was best to attack that one first he was a malignant brute. He stayed perched on Millie's shoulder, and kept looking at me and daring me to interrupt his gory feast, but the more he defied me the more determined I became. The only thing available to me was to replace her bitter memories with happy memories, but this was not easy with that beast trying all the time to keep the bad memories in place. They say there is no love like a mother's love and I made it very plain I was going to fight for Millie, they responded with hate and I attacked with love.

It was heartening to see the smile on Millie's face as I interrupted her terrible thoughts with happy thoughts. The demons were frantic they were rushing around trying to ensure their unhappy thoughts remained, while I worked hard to beat them at their own game. It was not easy they were well settled and Millie was totally receptive to them, it was ghoulish to see how hard they worked to keep Millie in subjection to their every whim. They would fly around her trying to shield her from me, at the same time trying to instill their thoughts in her mind. I on the other hand stuck doggedly interrupting their work much to their frustrated anger; it was just as well we were spirits because it would be a real tussle if we were not so inhibited.

One day much to my horror the Demon of Percy's adultery was demonstrating to her imagination just what he was up to now, the manner in which this was being achieved was so horrible. Millie was going into fits of anguish much to her demons joy and amusement. As I tried to interfere I found it almost impossible to get through to Millie! The image created was so explicit and clear that I could not break it no matter how hard I tried; the harder I tried the more the image expanded in the end I gave up. I was only making it worse, but I decided that was the demon we were going to get rid of first. The next day from the very start I had Millis imagination on pleasant things about her marriage and I never let up all day, no matter how that demon tried to interfere I continued,

It was nice to see Millie with a smile on her face for a change. I bought back memories of the children and how during her annual visit to the nursing home for two weeks she had such a wonderful rest. I reminded her of how loving Percy could be when they had no arguments going on. The demon was frantic as he tried to find his way back into her thoughts, but I persisted and would not let him break through. I continued on in this manner for over a month until I could see the demon weakening as he lost control over Millie, then one day just like that he was gone so that was one down and I was jubilant.

There were however a lot of angry looking demons eyeing me with an intense hatred, which is their natural condition so that was of no consequence to me. I had beaten one of their flock and they were waiting to see which one I was going to attack next. I chose the demon of suicide and what a din he set up as I started my work. Millie had when she was suffering from post natal blues, tried to swallow caustic soda and she had got some into her mouth before Percy caught her and stopped it, but she had already caused considerable damage.

Millie had been taken to hospital immediately but they had not been able to fully fix the problem. There was considerable damage to her throat and she still had difficulty swallowing, so much so that a lot of her food was liquid. The demon kept telling her that her food was poisoned, and everybody wanted to see her starve to death. Millie because she was suicidal anyhow embraced this idea with a childish appeal to let her die, and the demon kept saving her and making her go through the agony over and over. Again here was a scene that was unbelievable, Millie was pleading to be left to die, and her Demon kept restoring her to health all of the time. It was unbearable Millie kept pleading to die her demon kept reviving her, and enjoying the pantomime intensely.

I tried so hard to interfere but failed, hard as I tried I could find no way to create the will to live, and so I pulled back to try and figure out how to pursue the battle. Then in my mind I thought of a strategy, what if in Millie's imagination she were to die, and to see just what that would do to her family so I decided to try. First I had an image of all her Children pass before her eyes as if in full mourning for her, and at the same time I gave her an image of herself as dead. Then I, knowing Percy really did love her had his image as being totally devastated because she was gone. The visual effect and the effect on Millie were startling she woke from her reverie with a big smile on her face; I could see the formula was going to work.

Of course the demons were hysterical they could see another of their party was going to be lost, in another month suicide vanished too with a wail and a shriek of pure hatred at me. The remaining flock of demons was very agitated and trying to work out who was next, so I chose one at random guilt, and what a prime example he was. Millie had for years felt the guilt of what was a very disturbed life the guilt she carried was a very heavy burden to bear. The demon kept reminding her of things for which she felt real guilt like not being a good mother, and not spending time with her grandchildren even though she could not.

Once again I had a very determined adversary and he was a big ugly brute at that, but to be fair I had already beaten off two of the main offenders so Millie was now getting stronger; and I was getting more confident all of the time. It was about this time the Vietnam War was at its worst and the Americans were beginning to be beaten back, it was fascinating watching the determination with which the Viet Cong were gradually gaining the upper hand. I was not political but it was hard to see some of the atrocities committed in the name of freedom, and still believe the Americans were all about freedom. Day after day we received telecasts about what was happening and I could see it had a bad effect on Millie. Even though there was no comparison in her own life Millie still saw the pain of the villagers as they were burned and killed, as symptomatic of herself, to Millie her own children had been treated with horrible contempt. She felt guilty of being a half cast Maori married to a European and this was the hardest to take.

So the problem was how to defeat guilt no easy job under the circumstances and once again I was stuck for answers, while her tormenter carried on daily controlling her mind. This was a difficult one; I could not come up with an answer for several days as I sought the Lords guidance. One day the Lord spoke to me and said just prove the guilt is wrong show she is not guilty at all and she will recover very quickly. Millie believed that she was guilty because her family was rejected, they were cross bred to the Maoris and she carried the shame of that heavily.

It was not hard to remind her how happy the home was she had come from and there was no shame there. Percy's Mother also treated Millie as a second class person and this was hard for her to take. The children were sometimes treated badly, but not as much as Millie believed, her Mother in Law doted on Aloma the eldest daughter, but who would not the child was gorgeous from birth. The more I put positives into Millies head the more cheerful she started to become, and the more upset her demon became. I was becoming very positive myself as I could see it would not be long before another of that evil flock lost his place, so it was one day he was gone so that was four down looking good I thought. But the hard one was still to beat immolation or self destruction that was a real problem, in Millie's head if I could get rid of him we would be well on the way or so I thought.

Millie wanted badly to self destruct in every possible way and it was not easy to see how that could be dealt with, it was such a real desire on

Millie's part it was difficult to start to undermine her negative thoughts. Anyhow I started with Aloma and made it obvious it was so important to Aloma's well being for her Mother to be healthy and happy. Aloma was now a married woman with two children, and she was so concerned for her mother, she spent a big amount of time coming to the hospital, she was already beginning to sense an improvement in Millie's condition. I helped Aloma to realize the improvement was real and that Millie was beginning to change quite dramatically. Aloma's enthusiasm was spread to her mother and to the other sisters who constantly visited.

Even some of the staff could see that something was happening to Millie and the feeling was infectious throughout the ward. The positive reactions from everyone around began to affect her desire to self destruct, and to my delight she began to participate in everything around her. As this began to happen her destructive thoughts began to naturally vanish, much to the anger and frustration of her demon. As with the others his time was soon up and one day he was gone!

It was now really an easy matter to get rid of the rest of Millie's demons, they were quite minor by comparison, all of the bad ones were gone so the minor ones where already making as if to move on, and so now I had to be careful that Millie would not be exposed again, so now I had to start to prepare her for going home with Aloma.

While I did this the other demons began to lose interest and gradually they began to drift away and it was not long before Millie was free and a totally different person. It is not easy though to make sure there would be no new attacks. I knew real well that once left alone the demons would all be back with a vengeance, and I had to be sure Millie was well enough to withstand them.

I began to strengthen her on a diet of positive thoughts and dreams and gradually her whole personality changed, back to what she had been before she had fallen victim to Satan's ugly brutes.

Day after Day week after week I stayed with Millie and as she strengthened so her general demeanor changed, and it was becoming obvious. One day Aloma was taken aside and told that if her Mothers condition stayed good, she would be able to leave the hospital initially for short times and then they would see how she held up, if the prognosis stayed good well then she could stay with Aloma for good, released to Aloma's care. I stayed with Millie until she was released to Aloma's care, but I knew I would have to keep a very careful eye on Millie for quite a while, the crisis was still far from over I knew that very well.

Percy now leased a small shop in Albert St Auckland close in to the city, but in a fairly down market area, he was selling the usual bric a brac of a bookshop, newspapers etc; he was also living in the premises. There were quite good living facilities on the second floor, he was quite comfortable. This meant he was now close enough to constantly visit Millie at Aloma's home and made Millie a lot happier than she had been for many years. Originally Percy had been the one who had Millie committed to the home because of her irrational actions, he was delighted now that she was so much better.

Aloma now had the responsibility for her mother and she loved it .Her sisters helped as much as they could and visited Millie as often as possible. Millie's sons had now sold the farm and they also were more able to visit their mother. The mental stress Millie had suffered for many years, had taken its toll on her physical health; she began to have heart problems, aggravated by kidney failure.

Millie was quite naturally house bound, but Aloma tried as often as she could to take her on weekends out to visit her siblings, this seemed to energize her and she regained a little strength. Aloma tried everything she could to keep her mother interested in life, taking her out visiting and making sure her siblings and father visited more regularly their Wife and Mother.

Maria came up many times from Rotorua, and Ngaire and Susan were also constantly coming to visit their mother. Claire and Anne were really happy to see their sister, as usual only poor Winnie was left out, but she did come to the funeral when Millie died. The family finally had to accept their mother was slipping away, and they all knew she was dying. Although her kidneys had given her some pain she slipped away quietly with all of her children and Percy around her. Much to everyone's surprise Percy seemed to be lost when Millie died; he lost interest in living and died three months after Millie.

Millie was delighted to see me and of course we were both happy she had made it to heaven. My success with my family was becoming very exciting as now only Anne and Claire were still coming. Without question Millie applied to get into Christ's army and to both of us it was really great.

Chapter 8

―•⊷⊶•―

Winnie.

Here again there were demons everywhere, but strangely they were not being very successful. There was laziness, dirty home, ill kept children, and a father who spent all of his time in bed whenever he was not at work, and that was strictly eight hours per day. There was nothing consumed in excess. Alcohol and cigarettes were consumed only lightly, there was no hint of any immorality. There was sloth and laziness, and those demons were active but hardly very aggressive. To my complete surprise Winnie and her family seemed to give me the least problems of them all, I was both surprised and pleased.

Their Children were a sight to be pitied, and I could see more and more just how much work had to be done. The common thread was how the teachings Winnie had received as a child, had all been forgotten; it was amazing and so sad to see. Arthur and I had failed our children badly and they were reaping the whirl wind. I was treated with such derision by the demons, they all seemed to be saying all your children are dedicated to our God and he is King of this world, why don't you just give up, we have them very securely in our kingdom, and we are going to keep them, you are a failure.

Winnie and Albert would be the hardest of all my family to get through to, even as a child Winnie had been different from the other children. She had never responded to authority, Arthur and I had tried in every way to get through to Winnie, but she just would not listen. As a baby she was slow to

78

learn, slow to walk, slow to talk and slow to respond. As she was growing up Winnie did not get on with her sisters, but seemed to be ok with her brothers, although they sadly ignored her, she used to be happy so long as she could see one of the boys. At school she could not mix and her reports were very poor, it was obvious we had a problem child, but in those days isolated as we were there was little we could do, except to try and give her special attention. In looking back, I could now tell that so much was my fault. Winnie needed a mother who would devote far more time to her, we were too interested in getting out to the gum fields and Winnie was dragged along to work with the family.

Winnie was number four of the seven so she was expected to be able to work, but she never had any energy and was constantly being smacked by me for being lazy. It was so sad, the other six children and Winty were all very energetic. Winty, Anne, Dick and Murray were exceptional, their energy knew no bounds; Clare and Darby were good, but Winnie was the odd one out. When she left school she just wanted to lie around and do nothing, she did nothing around the house, and was really little use in the gum fields.

The only thing Winnie was interested in was boys, it was obvious we were going to have trouble with her before too long, so no boys except her brothers were allowed, anywhere around the house.

By the time we had to shift to Auckland Winnie was nineteen years of age and becoming a real handful, so it was with no regret that when we arrived she went to live with Clare and Anne. It was no surprise when Anne came to tell me Winnie had gone off with a man and was living with him. Naturally it was my job to kick up a fuss as her mother, but it was with relief when they got married and seemed to settle down in a small flat. Albert had a job in a sack factory sowing up sacks that had been damaged and he worked there all of his working life. Strictly eight hours a day and if he was lucky occasionally half an hour's overtime, but he did not want to do the extra time anyhow. They were not living far from Clare and myself so we went to visit occasionally at the start, but the home was so dirty and Millie and Albert so unkempt, we stopped going because it was to shameful for us to see, Clare was horrified at her sisters lack of home keeping skills and total laziness.

Winnie was just as fertile as Clare and Millie so children started to come straight away, eight in nine years, the eldest a boy, was called Arthur; named after his Grandfather. Winnie was totally unable to care for the baby so I offered to take him for my own provided he was left with me and not taken away as Winty had been. Winnie and Albert were both only too happy to let me have Arthur; they knew it had been hard on me when Winty was taken, so they promised they would never take him back.

For my part it was certain to me they would keep their word, Albert Ayers was no Percy Browne, and he only cared about having kids not looking after them. The next child was a girl, Patricia, and she was followed in quick succession by another seven others. Poor little Patricia, whenever we went to visit, her parents were in bed and Patty, as we called her was trying to look after the babies, as they came in quick succession, just like mine had. The home was always filthy and on occasion I tried to clean up a little in the hope Winnie would take a hint and do a bit of housework, she never did!

My need here was to try and work against the demons of sloth and laziness; I was at a loss how to work with them, for me this new type of problem it was hard to know how to start? It was obvious that Winnie loved her children, was it possible to shame her about the condition in which they were living? Albert was providing a steady income, in spite of him being ridiculed in his appearance; we had to admit he was a reliable provider. The only thing I could think of to do was again dreams, but what type of dreams would move Winnie, when nothing else ever had.

It was pointless to aim too high, it had to be an example Winnie could achieve, only Clare with her two pitiful little boys with eczema there seemed to be a small chance. What I did was show Winnie by way of dreams, that she was blessed in not having the troubles, that Clare was going through. It was easy to suggest that if she did not take better care of the kids, it was possible the same could happen to her. This affected Winnie immediately, she started taking more care of her brood and they started to look a lot better. Even Albert started to do a little work at home, so the easiest job of all with my children was quickly finished.

Albert to me was a marvel to behold, he was so skinny it was a miracle to me he could breed, but he seemed to do that very well, Winnie always seemed well satisfied with her life. Albert as well seemed quite happy, but to us he was a walking joke because he was so skinny, even Winty used to laugh when he sighted Albert walking to his work, he looked like some scraggy clothes walking down the road, but he kept his job. The job of a man is after all to feed his family, and to give him credit Albert did that for all of those years.

Winnie's family seemed to grow up fine and most quite energetic, so she must have passed on the normal Stephens genes that were a blessing to us all. All of the family loved Winnie, it was just that she had no energy and as a result was lazy. Albert was a different thing he was the family joke, sadly we all treated him with no respect, to my sons and Winty they wandered how he could keep walking and not break. The joke was they could hear Albert walking down the road, because he rattled like a walking skeleton would, poor Albert.

Winnie and Albert never did get to own a home, but they did get a Government home because they had so many kids, but they were happy with their lives and their children grew up ok and in some ways were better off with some of the other kids. For example, Millies and Darby's children had harder lives than the Ayers children had. Winnie and Albert both passed away in their early sixties, in spite of what we, her family had to say, they had a life that satisfied them, and in their own way they raised their children quite successfully.

For my part I had Arthur from birth and the little fellow turned out to be slightly retarded, he died at age 42 after a quiet but good life. Winnie was met when she arrived the same as I had been and she was admitted to heaven of course to my delight. When she entered heaven of course I was there to meet her and it was a joyous reunion. Winnie chose to join Christ's Army so she could work with her children as has been done by me. Again like me she was accepted and the last time we were together, she was winning the battle the same as I had done._

A long Journey home:

Written by Vincent Havelund

48 Short Stories

Introduction

This is the part of a series of stories that give examples of the life of the Maori Author they are written in such a way certain stories are applicable to different books he has written. As is common with many Authors because they write, a story 'fact or fiction' but behind their writings there is often glimpses of their own lives' In this Authors case this is often the case so that certain short stories are added to the end of each book, to demonstrate where some of the story may originate from. The biggest influence to his work is the Holy Bible which is the book most dear to him and affects his thoughts, therefore most influential in his writing. There are 120 short stories in the whole full cavalcade of his interesting and often diverse life._

Peanuts galore

August 1938:#1

It was cold outside that little slab house in Waihopo, the weather windy with rain sheeting down on that winters evening in August 1938. Inside it was snug and warm, the family gathered around the open hearth fire and enjoying each other's company. The house was small but a normal size for those times. There was three bedrooms one for Mum and Dad, one for the three brothers and another for the four sisters. The youngest Millie's Son slept in the room which was for Mum and Dad Stephens.

Dick and Millie were arguing Dick complaining loudly about the smallness of the meal he had been served. Millie was protesting loudly that all of the boys were just big and greedy. Darby and Murray were quiet although they still felt hungry, they knew their eldest Sister was unhappy and didn't want to be going to Auckland to work, so they were keeping quiet. Millie was looking to her younger Sisters for support, but they knew better than to be arguing with Dick. Millie was a naturally gifted cook, which meant she was left to do the main cooking for the entire family.

There was two sources of income, one was the little country store that Arthur owned and ran. He was also the local gum buying agent for an Australian paint company. His job was to buy the gum off the diggers (90% Maori the rest Chinese) and arrange shipment to Australia. Mary used to go out with all of the children including Winty, digging for Kauri Gum. This was hard back breaking work, but the only way the local Maoris' could earn a living although they all owned Maori land. The only one exempt from this work was Claire her job was on the fields alright, but looking after the

87

beloved Winty. Claire and Winty grew up as one but Claire was older by nine years.

Annie sixteen and Clare twelve YOA were too young to be bothered with the family niggles, they were too excited with the thoughts of the monthly dance that was due in ten days, and thinking about their new dresses that were being made.

Mother (Mary a full blooded Maori) and Father (Arthur a White Man) Stephens looked at each other and smiled contentedly. Millie's Son Vincent would be four years old on his next birthday 25th Oct 1938, his Father had been banished from the family in spite of vigorous resistance from Millie. It had been decided Vincent was to be raised by his Grand Parents, and Arthur had used his influence to get Millie a job as a cook at Karitane Hospital in Symonds St Auckland. Mary couldn't pronounce Vincent, in her poor English her pronunciation came out Winty. Winty's Father Bobbie Roberts was the youngest Son of one of Mary's Brothers, so his Parents Millie and Bobbie were first cousins. Bobby had been a trusted member of the extended Stephens, Roberts's families until the pregnancy had been revealed. The feisty Mary had expelled him from any mixing with her family; in her eyes she had been betrayed. Even 'Darby', who was a close friend of Bobbies, was suspected of having been complicit in the betrayal; he was being very quiet in the need to allay his Mothers wrath.

Any member of the Family, including Arthur who dared answer Mary back, or get out of line in any way received full punishment by being hit as she wielded her straw broom in mock anger. The only person Mary could really catch was Arthur, so many were the times he felt the whip of Mary's ire in substitution for one of the children. Of course that old straw broom couldn't hurt anyone, but it was a great game enjoyed by all, including Mary in her feigned anger.

Quite unexpectedly there was a commotion outside, and looking out Anne whooped "hey Aunt Olive and Uncle John are just arriving". Olive was Arthur's Sister and the only one for whom Mary tried to be courteous, but she dreaded those visits. Olive loved to buy chocolate peanuts from Arthur's shop. She used to buy the confectionery from Arthur every week, but there was a problem. Olive had no teeth so she couldn't eat the peanuts. She used to suck those lollies of all the chocolate, and save the peanuts which she would bring for Winty to eat, much to Mary's horror and disgust. Usually there was a rush to take Winty outside, or in some other way get him away from those peanuts and his loving Aunt Olive. Today was a problem, how was it to be worked, how could they get rid of those awful peanuts that Winty had tasted and loved so much. The answer was to send him to bed and make out he was asleep, then try to get rid of the visitors as quickly as possible. And so it was above Winty protestation he was rushed off to bed, before the visitors were ushered into the house. Claire was left to keep him quiet and Anne was to kick up a fuss about her dance dress; so the excuse to get rid of the guests could be accomplished quite quickly.

So the stage was set. Sure enough Olive had a big bag of sucked nuts, which she clutched in readiness to pass on to Winty. Anne had out her dress for the dance and Claire was keeping Winty quiet, but there was one big mistake. No one had allowed for Winty understanding what was going on, and there was no way he was going to give up those peanuts. Just as soon as he could hear that Olive was in the house and the nuts were there he let out an almighty bellow for Mary, there was no way out, he was awake.

By crikey those peanuts were good, that little fella gurgled and gooed and ate the lot, much to the families horror.

Mary never recovered from that, and for some reason Auntie Olive never again appeared with those wonderful pre sucked nuts._

Gone shopping

1941 (# 3)

This was a big event for a very spoilt little boy who thought it natural to get whatever he wanted, and was too young to know the truth. But like most of us life matures us all, those of us that had this experience were indeed blessed.

Boy oh boy! Winty was going out with the Big Kids and they told him they would take him shopping. They were all going to Woolies up in Karangahape Road just over from the top end of Queen St: Claire and Mum didn't know the Big Kids had told Winty it was to be a secret. It was so exciting! First they were all going to the movies and Winty had sixpence all for himself. Three pence was for the movies two pence for lollies and a penny for an ice cream cone. Gosh it was a really big thing to be going out without Mum and Aunty Claire. The big day was here and Winty was up early ready to go, you know what they were going to that big place Mum and Aunty Claire had taken him to the Civic Theatre? That place where the piano rose up out of the floor and the man played music gosh this was a big day he was going there again.

Winty had not long ago come to live in the city with his Mum and Aunt and he still didn't know much about his new home and surroundings. For him to be going out with anyone other than his Mum and Aunt was just so exciting. This five year old for the first time in his life, he was going out alone and he was a very spoilt little boy!

Most of the other youngsters were from ten to fifteen years of age and were in some way related to little Winty, usually Mum wouldn't let him out of her sight. The Big Kids had reassured her they would take good care of him, and not let him out of their sight. This is why it was so exciting and the Kids had promised to take him shopping, where you didn't have to have any money to buy things. They were going to buy him lots of things with no money, but he had to keep it as a big secret and not tell his Mum and Aunty, because big people couldn't shop without any money.

The movie was great and that piano (it was a Wurlitzer organ) was like magic winding its way out of the floor, and the man was playing and waving to all of the kids. It was the school holidays the Civic was packed out with kids and Winty was so excited he was with the kids, but he had money for himself, his Aunty Claire had given him sixpence and told him how to spend it at the lollie shop. She need not have worried he was young, but even then the kids couldn't get his money, especially if his beloved Aunt had given it to him, she had to work for it you know!

Anyhow the movies were over and they were going shopping. Finally they got to the big shop and it had different toys and lollies everywhere, Winty had on a coat with big pockets. Gee it was such fun the kids were filling up his pockets, and his trouser pants as well gosh.

This was really great Winty wandered if he could find this place by himself and come shopping alone. The others were going to take some off him when he got outside. That was only because he was so little. The older kids had told him that; so why should they get some of it when it's me that's allowed to keep this stuff. Not only that they were choosing everything and most of it was no use to Winty, he only wanted those pretty lollies anyhow.

Ok the Big Kids said that's all he could have so they would wait for him outside, while he carried the stuff out, then they would all share what he had. This is funny why should they wait outside and leave him to carry everything out then they wanted to keep most of it, oh well just this once, but not anymore.

Then as Winty was walking out the door a big man said to him, "where are you going Sonny?"

"My name isn't Sonny its' Winty and I am going home with my shopping why do you want to know you have nothing to do with me?" Winty said haughtily.

"What about all of those things you have in your pockets do you have the money to pay for them, because you will need a lot of money?" the man said with a smile.

"No I don't need money mister because I am only five so no and goodbye, as soon as my Mum lets me come I will be back because this is a nice shop giving kids like me goods for nothing. All of my friends are waiting for me outside and they want most of the stuff that they have given me. Next time when we do come it will be with my Mum, and then she will tell me what to buy for nothing. Don't you think this is a very nice shop for little kids like me?"Winty said with a big smile.

"Sonny you are the smallest and cheekiest thief that has ever come here now give me those lollies and toys back, and then bugger off before the Policeman comes for you".

"No you can't have my shopping whats a policeman and whats a thief, no you bugger off before I get my friends to bash you up, now bugger off mister," said a little Winty who was close to tears by then.

Needless to say by the time that big man took Winty home and told Mum and Aunty Claire he had been shopping with no money, there was no more going out with the Big Kids, but whats a policeman and whats a thief? That man got Mum to take Winty's shopping of him even though he cried really hard, and she didn't let him go shopping again.

The Cookie Jar

1940: #4

Winty's Mum was really his grandmother, which of courses why he was so spoiled._

Winty was at home with his Mum and she was baking cookies, oh boy he would have to be good so he could have some when his Mum had finished. May be if he was real good he would be able to have some to share with his friends those big kid who had taken him shopping, and also one or two for his pet dog. But his dog was so big and greedy he could eat the lot easily by himself and leave none for Winty.

He had been able to get the bowl that his mum used to mix up the cookies and he had scraped it clean, gosh it had been so yummy, but that had only made him hungrier for the cookies. Mum had finished her baking and had set those cookies on the table to cool! She had told Winty not to touch them, but the smell was so nice he could not wait any longer?

Mum was out on the lawn sitting in the sun talking to a neighbor friend, and waiting for the cookies to cool off. Sneaking in to the table Winty took one off the plate, being careful to leave no crumbs, and ate it. Boy it was so yummy!

After he had eaten one he felt even hungrier so he took another and then another, then his pet dog came in so he gave him one or two! Suddenly when he went back for another there were no more on the plate, oh my! 'He thought'. How could they have all vanished just like that? What would Mum say about the missing cookies, she might be angry, where is that greedy dog he must have eaten them while Winty was not looking? Where is that naughty dog, he is such a greedy boy? Winty knew he could not be trusted! Maybe if he put the plate away and wiped the table where those cookies had been, Mum would forget them and she might even bake another lot that would be really nice. Then he could share them with the big kids, but he would make sure the dog got no more, he was so naughty!

Winty began to feel a little funny in his tummy so decided he might be best to lie down on his bed for a while! He had just been lying down for a little while when he heard his Mum come inside, then he could hear his name being called. Maybe she had seen the plate was missing off the table! Maybe if she noticed she might know the dog had eaten the cookies, he was a very hungry dog and was always stealing food? Winty decided to pretend he did not hear his Mum calling and that he could pretend he had not been inside all day as he had?

But then suddenly Winty began to feel real sick in his tummy, and he could not understand what was wrong, surely it couldn't be the cookies, he had he thought only eaten a few? Oh my then he began to feel worse and then really bad, his tummy was really sick now! What could be wrong he just wanted the sick feeling to go away?

His Mum's voice kept coming to him as she called his name, but she was beginning to sound angry! That dog must be in trouble or else why would she be angry? But his stomach seemed to get sicker and sicker he would have to go and tell his Mum, but he would just wait until that naughty dog was caught?

Maybe those cookies were not so nice after all. He started to feel sick at the thought of them, it was just as well he had left them to the naughty dog and only eaten a few. Then he began to wonder if his dog had a sick tummy too, he must have, there had been a lot of cookies on that plate, the dog would be real sick by now.

Mummies voice kept getting louder, why didn't she look for that naughty dog there was no need to get angry, after all she could so easily make some more? But Winty did not want any he decided he didn't like cookies at all! If just eating a few had made him feel so sick, there must be something wrong with Mums cookies. Now he could hear that noisy dog barking, he must be so pleased that he had such a good feed of Mums cookies! He was such a naughty dog, he Winty would tell Dad when he got home what the dog had done, eaten Mums cookies.

It would never have happened if Mum had not sat outside talking to the neighbor lady! That lady was always talking and holding Mum up from her work. Winty knew that because he had heard Mum say we were talking today and I almost forgot the dinner, 'yes Dad would understand'.

Suddenly his Mum walked into the room and gosh she was looking so angry! Winty wondered if she was sick too, maybe she had eaten too many cookies as well. But Winty felt too sick to tell his mum about the dog, anyhow she must have eaten cookies too that's why she was looking so angry? Now Winty's tummy hurt so much that he started to cry, and convulse in pain. He forgot all about that naughty dog and all about Mum eating her own cookies, all he could think about were the few he had eaten!

Gosh he was thinking as his tummy throbbed thank goodness I didn't eat too many it would have been really bad. Yes he would tell his mum not to cook anymore cookies cos maybe they would kill the dog next time. Suddenly the look on Mums face changed, she must have realized that Dog had eaten all of the cookies thought Winty, as he convulsed into another tummy pain? Suddenly Mum was holding Winty and hugging him and crooning to him asking his if he was all right!

Winty wanted to tell her how the Dog had eaten the cookies, but then decided why get my dog into trouble, Mum must have forgotten about the cookies anyhow?

Winty at the Butchers shop

1941: #5

There no trusting relations, especially if they don't like ya, best to stay back and wait for my Aunty.

Winty had been taken to the Butchers shop by his cousins the Reid Kids, they didn't want to take him, but he had tried so hard Mum had insisted he be allowed to go. Then they took him up one way but when they started to go home they wanted to go another way. No Winty said you aren't taking me there, that's not the way we came we must go back the same way. Look you snotty nosed little brat we are going this way, if you don't want to come well stay behind we don't care. I am not going that way you can go where you like, but you can't make me go there when it's the wrong way.

It had been a big day Winty's cousins the Reid's lived in Cook St which was the way the children had come, but they wanted to go back down Union St and he knew they hadn't come that way. The Reid's didn't like Winty because he was young and very spoilt, and even at that age had a way of doing what he wanted, not what others wanted him to do. They both knew that only his Mum and or his Aunty Claire could control Winty, and they didn't want anything to do with him. Their Father when they complained had told them to behave and they had to be good to Winty because he was their first cousin, and he wasn't going to argue with his sister Aunty Mary to hell with that!

Anyhow on the day in question, the eldest Reid who was twelve YOA didn't like it; when Winty had forced them to take him with them up to Mr Kneebone's butcher shop. They didn't dare defy Mary or Claire Stephens,

96

but when Winty played up they had no more patience, leave the little brat there they agreed between them.

The Reid's went home and told nobody they had left Winty alone up at Mr. Kneebone's shop, 'to hell with him', they were too frightened to go tell Mary Stephen's so they just left him alone. Winty was not frightened but very defiant, he wouldn't shift for anyone.

Back at home Aunt Claire and Mum were both worrying about Winty, where he was and why wasn't he home by now? Those Reid's were old enough surely he was ok, but that little bloke may have been too much for those two Reid boys to look after. Maybe you better go around to Reid's Clarela said Mum Stephens he may still be there, but they wouldn't play with him he is too young for them.

Ok Claire went around to the Reid's their home was about one kilometer away, but there was no one home or at least no one answered the door, and by this time there was much worry for Winty. Claire went home and got a big blast from her Mum, why you home you plurry ting? Where is my Winty you plurry finda him and hurry up quick, or you getta da broom you find him Clarela donta you comea home until you do.

Meantime up at the Butcher shop Winty was just fine Mr. Kneebone was feeding him lollies, and he was happily playing around just outside the shop. The family was well known they bought their meat off Mr. Kneebone; and he liked all of the Stephens clan.

The Butcher was happy to keep Winty entertained he knew Claire would come sooner or later; he knew also she would be in trouble with that old[1] Sheila if the little bloke wasn't found. 'Mum Stephens had made it plain many times who was the boss at home, and Mr. Kneebone really liked that old Maori woman'.

Meantime Aunt Claire was at her wits end, where was the little brat she would' smack his spoilt arse when she found him'. Back she went to the Reid's but still no answer, Claire was furious what the hell have those damned Reid kids done, she knew they didn't like Winty but surely they wouldn't hurt him. 'She also knew that Winty would not obey those boys if they said or did the wrong thing hell what was she to do'?

'There was still no answer from the Reid's Claire was becoming frantic, and poor old Mum Stephens was almost throwing a fit where isa my Winty wata dey do with him if dey hurta him I sure hurta dem is dey hiding it no good dose plurry tings be no good tell Reid I be coming to see him and I basha his silly head he be a plurry fool'.

Finally Father of the boys 'Reid Reid' was home when Claire went there again, where are your boys she asked him?

"Why just outside whats wrong why do you want them? What have they done now the little brats are always into mischief." he said in a very sour voice.

"Well Mum is very upset with you Uncle and wants you to come to our house so she can talk to you, she is real angry. Your boys took Winty to the butcher shop five hours ago and he isn't anywhere to be found, she is at home really screaming, you had better go and see her and take your sons with you I will go home and wait with her."

'Yes I know what Mary is like she has done me over before, we will be there as soon as I get those boys and their Mother, tell Mary we are coming Claire'.

'When Reid arrived with his boys and Wife, Mary started wata you do'a with my Winty you plurry poys you betta not have hurt him where is he'?

"We left Winty at the Butchers shop because he wouldn't come with us, we didn't do nothing to him." said two very frightened boys.

"You what left him at the shop and never came to tell me you two little brats he had better be still there and ok, or you two are in trouble!" screamed Claire with Mary carrying on in pigeon English in the background.

Claire rushed up to the shop to be greeted by a very happy Winty full of Mr Kneebone's Lollies, "hello Aunty why have you been so long I have been waiting for you? Those Reid boys left me behind, I don't like them anymore." He said as he gave a very relieved Aunt Claire a big kiss, and no she never smacked his backside she wouldn't dare, he would have told Mum.

Living on a Farm

Why do you only have two teats when the cows have four Mum, don't you wish you had four as well'?

Winty and his parents were going to live on a farm in Titirangi just thirty kms north of Auckland. His Mum and Dad had taken up a share milking contract on a medium sized farm, milking one hundred and twenty cows for cream was the main work. But growing Pigs, a small flock of sheep for meat lambs and five acres for a mixed crop was work to be done also! The soil was very rich and the return was high for quite a small property which could easily be run by two men and casual help, when harvesting hay and other crops? There were over 80 hectares of dairy land and another hundred of high sheep country. Winty had lived in a rural setting as a baby but had not been around animals before, this was why he was so excited and kept up a constant chatter on their journey to the farm, that first day. Winty had a pet kelpie dog called Shep, and he wanted to know if there would be other dogs living with them at the farm.

His Dad had said there were two dogs and when asked what animals there were had answered that there were 120 cows, 40 calves, 15 sows with assorted litters, 500 sheep plus about 450 lambs, 2 horses 10 goats, 2 great big bulls, one Boar and 20 Rams. Gosh Dad Winty enthused can I help to look after all of those animals, and can Shep work with the two dogs that are at the farm already? Both parents gave their little Son a hug and agreed he would be able to help, and Shep would be taught to help as well? Both had learned to be careful how they spoke to Winty, they knew he was apt to take things they said too literally, and hear only what he wanted to hear?

They arrived at their new home in the late afternoon the contract was not due to start for another two days, but Mr. Stephens wanted to move in early to orient his family before he started work? Without any wasted time Winty was running around his new home, (it was a huge farm house) and out playing with Shep and the two new dogs. His father had asked if he (Winty) wanted to ride around to see the farm riding on the horse drawn sledge, in the morning which of course he did. The animals and equipment had to be checked out before the contracted transfer time, it was quite a big job and would take a full day's work. Winty's Mum was going out to; she was a skilled farm worker and was going to help in the cow shed milking cows in the morning; and on the weekends. The intent was to save wages, but she loved farm work and was looking forward to the future.

The next morning the two big horses were harnessed and hitched to the sledge before Winty woke up, and then after breakfast they were off. Oh it was such an exciting adventure, and Winty had the two week school holidays to get used to his new home, today it was to be riding on the sledge. Both parents were standing as the sledge started off behind the horses, but Winty's Mum had a firm hold of his shoulders. No don't do that said Winty this is easy the horses are very slow aren't they? I don't need you to hold me gosh we are hardly moving, this was said as the horses just ambled along at sledge speed. Winty was right he found it easy to balance as they were riding along, but without thinking his Dad called to the horses whoa there and they stopped. Crikey Winty seemed to keep going and finished up under the back of the horses feet, hey called his dad you said you could ride without help?

Winty stood up brushed down the dirt he had got from the fall and looking rather sheepish stepped back onto the sled, but this time sat down. No worries said his Mum there will be lots of funny things happening before you get used to your new life. Almost everyone does that when first they ride a sledge, Dad just forgot to warn me so we could have held you, and you will slowly learn to ride properly.

Meantime Shep a Kelpie was in his natural environment and frolicking around very happily, he had his tongue hanging out and yelping to Winty in his happy way. The first animals they went to count were the Pigs, crikey that was exciting! The Momma pigs were huge and they were lying down with lots of little ones running around trying to get at the teats for a drink of milk so Mum said. Each Momma pig had babies of different, sizes, but all the Mums were lying down and all of the young were trying to drink.

Crikey said Winty looking at his Mum, just as well you had only me to feed you would be too small to feed the dozens those mums have to feed. Then they went to the other pigsties and there were lots of bigger pigs running around with no Mums. These ones were eating from troughs and drinking from water nipples on the wall, gosh said Winty how old are those ones Dad? Oh said his Dad with a shrug, about 4-5 months they will be full grown soon some are full grown already, see those ones there they are full grown and around 6 months old. Gosh said Winty they must have eaten a lot to get to that size so fast, just imagine if I could grow that fast I would be as big as you are now Dad.

Yes Son that's true, but those fully grown ones will be going to market any day soon, and some butcher will buy them. Others will turn them into Bacon and Ham and the Mums will buy those products from the Supermarket, and then they will be eaten.

Gosh said Winty I think it's better to be a little boy and just grow up slowly, nobody will eat me! I think it will be better if we should eat the butcher don't you agree Dad?

Mum and Dad laughed but each wandered privately what mischief their Son would soon be getting into as he learned to be a farm boy, it was their only worry!

Winty dancing with pigs

Gosh pigs don't want o do anything you want them to do, they only want to sleep eat or dance!

The family had settled into the farm and now it was time to send a flock of pigs to market. Winty wanted to be part of everything, so now he was going to take his dog Shep and show Dad just how good they were together He and Shep! He knew where the pigs were to go and he knew the ones that were going, so off they went just Winty and Shep, his Dad would be so proud? What a great surprise his Mum and Dad would get after milking they would not have to drove the pigs anywhere, it would all be done, Winty was already proud of Shep because they were both doing it together! Dad had called Shep stupid a few days ago, while they were trying to separate out a neighbor's bull that had got in with the herd. The other two dogs kept separating the bull just as Dad wanted and Shep kept chasing it back, after he had done this several times dad had yelled at Shep, go away you stupid mutt?

Winty and Shep arrived at the pigs pens soon after milking started they could hear the machines going brmp, brmp, brmp so Mum and Dad would be very busy now? Opening the gates of the pens and waking the pigs up, was the first step. The pigs all got up and started to squeal with delight, they all thought they were going to get an extra dinner so they would not go through the open gate? Every time one did go through it would quickly come back because it didn't want to be separated from the others, there were twelve in the group. Round and round the pen they went Shep was useless they just ran straight at him, poor dog, he had never even seen a pig before?

Finally after the pigs realized there was no extra dinner for them, they decided look there's an open gate maybe there's some food out there so off they went straight through! Aha thought Winty now we are off to market, but then the real fuss started, each pig wanted food, but each one went looking in different places. Shep would try to drive one back the way they wanted and whoosh it would run the opposite way. Winty would run and chase them, but they would stop, look at him as if saying ok now where is that food now hurry up we are hungry. If you have no food why did you wake us up, let's go back and let us go back to sleep?

Winty was getting angry and started to shout at the pigs, then he started to shout at Shep, it was no use they kept going round and round in circles. The more Winty shouted the more inquisitive the pigs became, they came closer to him and sniffed him as if to say, does he want us to eat him. My he is just a little fellow he may taste quite good, but why does he want to be eaten no that's not it; he is just doing a dance to show us what to do.

So the pigs started to run around and dance. Each end went in different directions front to the left back to the right then reverse it, there were pigs dancing all over the place one two three, one two three. Crikey this was good so they started to squeal as well, one two three oink,oink they loved it, they were going round and round doing the pig dance. Winty and Shep well they were dancing too stupid pigs, stupid pigs and Shep was going Woof, Woof, Woof they were all in perfect harmony doing the pig dance. It started with a slow waltz, but as it get faster and faster it got up to rock and roll, and the pigs changed steps, instead of left right, it became right left, and they loved it. More, more they squealed faster, faster oink, oink no don't slow down oink, oink more please more we are awake now, there is no extra dinner so let's dance, we just love this?

Winty was very upset he stopped running he was puffed out, the pigs weren't puffed out though they came back and started to sniff him again, yes you smell alright but no we don't eat little boys, hey let's dance some more. The pigs started going round and round by themselves back to the left, front to the right now reverse that, one two three, more, more no it's better if you dance with us so they stopped, and smelt Winty some more.

Then Shep decided he was going to dance with the pigs, he started to bark and go round in circles with the pigs one two three woof, woof went Shep yes the pigs went round as well one two three oink, oink. It was great fun so Winty forgot he was trying to take the pigs to the stockyards, he started to run around as well, one two three hey, hey they were all having a great time. Round and round, oink, oink woof, woof hey, hey it was great the twelve pigs the little boy and his dog taking the pigs to market, or was it the pigs taking the boy and his dog for a dance?

Meantime milking was finished, and the cows had all gone back to their day paddock for breakfast, but Winty had forgotten about that he was busy dancing with the pigs. Suddenly the machines stopped chuffing and all went silent, Winty and Shep stopped dancing, but the pigs didn't they kept it up oink, oink.

Suddenly Mum and Dad were standing there asking Winty and Shep what they were doing. When Winty explained they burst out laughing much to Winty's surprise. Here said Dad watch this, getting a bucket he filled it with pig grits, and started calling here pig, pig. Come on lets go so walking in front of the pigs he started to walk towards the stockyards, the pigs stopped dancing immediately and followed Dad, ?

That's good look it's an extra dinner just what we wanted, so they all followed Dad eating as they went right into the stockyards. Shep stood watching and lolling his tongue in exhaustion, Winty thought gosh that's easy, and the pigs well they stopped dancing and Dad threw them the rest of the corn grits that were left in the bucket. The pigs were real happy they ate the extra breakfast and then lay down and went to sleep.

The Cow

Mate you havta watch those cows when we are feeding them on turnips, they can shit 20 meters without even trying just don't get in the line of fire.

Life on the farm for a five year old boy was wonderful and Winty was into and learning all he could, he loved being with all of the animals. One day he asked his Dad, why does the cow poo not smell but the pigs do, and why do the calves poo come out yellow Dad? Well Son the cows only eat grass and that doesn't smell, so the only time they smell is if they are eating something different like say turnips, or silage? Pigs are like humans they are omnivorous, which means they eat meat and vegetables, and calves only drink milk that's why the yellow color? Winty had so many questions, like all little boys he wanted to know everything, sometimes Dad got tired of answering what seemed like endless questions. But Winty kept it up why do cows have four teats and goats only two, why do pigs have two rows of teats, on and on it went day after day. At night in bed sometimes Dad would say to Mum that Kid has me beat, he gets me so tired, questions as soon as he gets home from school it's what, what, what? Don't worry Mum would say he will only keep it up until he is about fifteen, then it will be no, no, no, or yes, yes, yes.

Sometimes Winty was allowed in the cow shed to watch, but too often he would get in the way, so it was not often he could get where he most wanted to be in with the cows? The winter was progressing and grass was a little short so it was time to add to the daily rations, hay, silage, turnips and sugar beet it was all a lot of extra work. Unlike other countries grass was so prolific in NZ only a limited time of the year was extra feed given to the bovine animals (cattle). Sheep never get extras and goats were just considered to be a nuisance anyhow. Mum and Dad kept and milked the few goats just to make goats cheese which they both loved. Winty was learning to know the difference, why he asked don't you milk the sheep Dad and what about the lady horse.

Because we in NZ don't eat sheep cheese and we certainly don't eat horse cheese, horses are like dogs they are workers, said Dad with a grimace. Here we go thought Dad it will carry on now until I can get into the cowshed out of the way, praise God for milking time! Mum just stood out of the way and smiled to herself, she was very proud of their little Son, and she knew how to dodge the questions, she pretended not to know the answers just said I don't know ask your Dad? Winty really loved his Mum, he knew he had the best Mum in the world she didn't seem to know much, but she was the best Mum in the whole world.

Anyhow the cows were on turnips and the milk was very strong, but because their farm was on cheese supply it didn't matter how strong the milk was the cheese factory didn't care, there was no effect on the cheese? Winty had managed to wangle his way into the cow shed and was as usual being a nuisance to his Dad, while his Mum smiled wisely, and the questions were flowing. Why he asked are the cow's pooing all over the place tonight? Do they all have a stomach ache, like when we eat to many cookies'? No said Dad it's because we are feeding turnips just at present that always gives them the runs for a few days, but they will settle down after a little while, they love turnips.

If we eat turnips will we stink too Dad asked Winty? Yes said Dad with a resigned shrug but I don't like turnips nor does your Mum so we won't be eating them, if we have too many we will feed the surplus to the pigs then there will be a real stink?

There was a cow standing up at the other end of the shed facing away from Winty, when she suddenly lifted her tail to poo. As she was starting to poo she gave a big cough, and the poo seemed to spurt out of her in a great arc, it landed all over Winty from head to foot he was covered in turnip flavored cow poo. Oh crikey what a mess, his Dad couldn't help himself he just burst out laughing, Winty was bewildered he was drowned in poo, Mum rushed over to the hose and was hosing Winty down with water. The poor old cow was horrified she was walking around shaking her head, and seemed to be saying who has shit all over that poor little fellow, who would do that?

The other cows were looking at the culprit and seemed to be saying to her, why do you have to shit everywhere you silly old fool? We will all be blamed as

Silly old moo but it's only you, go away we are so ashamed of you, and by the way you stink what have you been eating anyhow?

The old bull he was out in the bull pen and could see what the cow had done, he just started to growl in his heavy bull language. Don't send her out to me he seemed to say, she might shit all over me too, no send her straight out and don't give the old fool any more turnips. He stood there shaking his head and looking very disgusted.

By the time Winty had been cleaned down he had to go back to the house have a shower and change his clothes, but by time he left the shed Winty was laughing as well? From then on when the cows were eating turnips there was no way Winty would go near that cow shed at milking time!

Sheep and Lambs

The best time of the year as the small farmers work together again.

It was shearing time and Winty and Dad had driven their little flock to the shearing shed to wait for the shearers, who were due in the next day. Several farmers were bringing their flocks in and were penning them up in separate pens, so they did not get mixed up. In this way there was enough work for the shearers to stay about two weeks, and earn enough money to make it worthwhile coming? The sheep had to be kept separate and so did the fleeces so that each farmer got his full entitlements. The farmers all work together to do the laboring work in this way they cut their costs, and those with a few more sheep than the others, their families supply the dinners.

The shearers and fleecies are paid for each sheep the going contract rate, and if there was not enough sheep to shear they would not come, the travel made it not worth while unless there was a minimum of several thousand full fleece sheep! Winty loved it even better than crop time when the hay and silage is being made. Winty was a little older now over six years of age, and Shep was learning to work the cattle properly he was becoming quite a good cattle dog and really loved the work.

After Dads flock had been finished without thinking he had asked Winty if he could drove the flock back to a fresh paddock with plenty of short grass. Winty joyfully said he could and as soon as their sheep were finished he left with the little flock, and on the way collected the lambs so the Ewes, (Mother sheep)and their young were reunited.

There were three things Dad had forgotten in his hurry to keep up with his share of the work in the shearing shed. Shep was proving to be a cattle dog so use less with sheep! Cattle dogs make little noise but will rush in and bite the heels of cattle when they are not being obeyed by the stock, sheep dogs are noisy and drove with their noise. A good sheep dog when he knows the master, will know by the whistle where to go, and will just make a lot of noise when changing direction, but lie on its belly and watch when the flock is going the right way? The Ewes being freshly shorn (A sheep's haircut) and free of their winter fleece are naturally frisky, and with their young lambs beside them will be more frisky than usual.

Anyhow Winty, Shep and the Ewes with their lambs were off and they were going the wrong way, so Winty called to Shep catch em boy and pointed the way. Shep rushed in like a good cattle dog, got close then rushed in and bit a few Ewes on their heels, there was hell to play, the flock scattered all over the place. Lambs were bouncing up and down Ewes were running around and the leaders just stopped and started to eat. NO, NO Winty yelled at Shep over there he said pointing again, so Shep did it again just as the flock had settled down again? Hi ho the lambs were jumping again and loving this game, how high do you want us to jump and how often hi ho and off we go. Their mothers the Ewes this time, turned and looked at Shep as if to say make up your mind you idiot and stop biting our heals.

Crikey Winty thought this is a great game so he joined in and so did Shep! The Lambs were jumping and the Ewes had their heads down and were trying to catch Shep, but he was trying to get at the old girls heels so it was a merry go round. Winty was running and trying to jump as high as the lambs, Shep was still trying to bite the Ewes heels and the Ewes were trying to butt Shep all in all it was better than droving pigs. Round and round they went like a merry go round, but they were moving in the general direction, even if it was only very slowly.

As they moved forward going round and round, the newly shorn Ewes decided to take no notice of Shep and just ignored him; they started to jump up and down like their lambs. Shep thinking now he had a chance rushed into a Ewes heels just as she jumped, and she landed right on the point of his nose.

Yike, yike, yike wailed Shep loudly! Oh is that what you want thought the Ewes so of they went just the way Winty wanted, with the lambs running and jumping beside their mothers. Round and round ran Shep yelling Yoik, Yoik struth that hurt Yoik, Yoik. The flock was now moving perfectly just as wanted, a sheep dog could not have done better, Yoik, Yoik. The flock was now moving so fast that they were back in the right paddock in record time? Winty and Shep had done a great job even if by accident?

That night after milking when Winty was telling his parents what had happened and how Shep had done such a great job, his Dad started to laugh out loud. Mum as usual just hugged her little boy and kissed him all over his face.

Great work Winty said his Dad you have done what we could not have done, driven sheep with a cattle dog that has to be a real victory, neither you're Mum or me could have done that? Winty was in heaven! I love farming he was thinking, when I grow up there will be lots of sheep and pigs for droving and cows for milking oh what a lucky boy I am, and Shep is such a smart dog fancy that a dog for sheep and cows, boy he is so smart.

Winty was so proud of Shep he could work with both cattle and sheep! None of the other dogs could do that Yoik, Yoik.

Shep the cattle dog

1942: #10

No you don't drove sheep with a cattle dog and you don't drove cattle with a sheep dog, and that household pet you have down there sonny, leave him at home he will be just a bloody nuisance is it really a dog or does it just smell like one?

Winty had been asked by his Dad to go down and open the gates, so the milking cows could get through, and they would slowly amble their way up to the milking shed. Winty knew some of the cows, but most of them had never really seen him and certainly they did not know Shep, but even worse Shep didn't know them. So far he had got to know the pigs, the Ewes and their Lambs, but had only worked with the neighbor's beef cattle, a different type all together than milking cows? Beef cattle are not used to being handled by people and hate dogs, when a dog starts to work them they will lash out with their hind legs, when the dog comes close. A good cattle dog will get in close grab hold of a hind leg, and hang on as the animal bucks and kicks, then let go as the animal runs instead of kicking. Finally when the herd is moving the right way the cattle dog will run round and round barking, but never as noisily as a sheep dog? They aren't like sheep dogs that run around and make a big noise, then lay down on their tummies on the ground when the flock is moving properly. Milking cows are used to being handled and like people, they will walk up to strangers and try to smell them, mill around walking slowly even the dog doesn't upset them unless like Shep, they are untrained?

On the day Winty was asked to open the gates it was just a very simple job, and Winty now six YOA was proud to do as his Dad had asked. Off he went with Shep trailing along as they always did, both young and happy. Shep was now just a little over eighteen months old which in human terms was nearly eleven years old? They arrived at the last gate and as they always do, the cows were standing waiting for Dad or Mum to open the gate! The usual pecking order applied the boss cows at the front, the others in order of seniority depending on how many calves they had born, and the first calf heifers last.

The old Sheila's (cows) have the right of way so they get milked first, and are back out of the milking shed first, they don't have to wait the youngsters do the waiting in the queue, it's the established cow order? Neither Shep nor Winty knew anything of cow proto col; they had just been asked to open the gates all the way up to the cowshed. They had come down and opened all of the gates on the way, now they were opening the last gate so the cows could walk up at their own pace, as Dad had asked.

As soon as the gate was opened the old girls instead of walking away stopped to sniff Winty, as if to say hello little boy whose baby are you? Then they looked at Shep and seemed to be saying, good day you ugly little mutt where the hell did you come from? We don't like ugly mutts like you shoo now go away, you stink just like all your kind, real stinky you lot are. To drive the point home they put their heads down and lumbered after Shep shaking their horns quite forgetting they no longer had horns? Shep put his tail between his legs, and tried to get close to Winty for protection, but the old girls would not allow that, they wanted Shep and they were going to horn him real bad, or that was the intent.

Suddenly they got too close and Shep got angry so he took off after an old cows hind heel, he latched on and hung on with his jaws locked in place! But now the cows were frightened Moo, Moo they all bellowed, let go there ya ugly little brute let go we say, so they were all trying to get that ugly little brute. Winty was yelling the cows were mooing and Shep was hanging on for the ride it seemed. Then suddenly Shep had enough, he let go and ran as fast as he could away from those stupid cows, off he went down the paddock with the heifers after him.

All the young cows were off udders shaking from side to side, milk squirting out all over the place, and they were going Moo, Moo, we are going to butt you right up your ugly butt they seemed to say. Shep was yelling bow wow bow wow leave me alone you silly cows! I aint done nothing why are you all chasing me? Winty was yelling for Shep but Shep had no time to listen to Winty, those young cows were close and he wasn't happy his tail was between his legs, and he was as frightened as he had never been, in his young life.

The older cows had forgotten Shep by now, they were walking towards the cow shed, only the young heifers were still chasing him, they were even younger than Winty, so they were enjoying themselves immensely. Jumping around shaking their heads they seemed to be laughing and playing as they ran.

Suddenly Shep finally got a bright idea he jumped through a fence, and the chase was over! Even the heifers the smallest in the herd could not fit between the wires, so they stopped, lowered their heads and kept shaking them they seemed to be saying, now don't come back you dirty little mutt cos we won't forget ya and next time we will catch you? Now having done their bit to protect their herd's honor, they walked after the senior cows with happy looks on their faces. Winty was sure they were saying, that fixed them two, now what do you want little boy, go home to your Mum?

When Winty told Dad what had happened, he laughed and said milking will be quick tonight, the old cows will be excited and let their milk down easily. It sounds as if the heifers have lost half of theirs in the paddock! Never mind they don't have much this year they will be in full production next season, after they have their second calf?

As for Shep he wasn't seen again until the next morning, and he was still not looking very happy!

Dreaming

1942: #11

This being a farmer is so much fun, but it's been such hard work today, I am going to be a farmer like my Dad when I grow up. My farm will grow Pigs and Sheep and lambs that jump and Cows that Poo, gosh it will be good to grow to be as big as Dad and be a farmer like him?

Winty was very tired that night it had been a big day at school, and when he got home, Dad had asked him to go and open the gate to the cow's paddock so they could come up by themselves for milking. There had been an incident with Shep when he got amongst the cows, but that had been fixed, and the cows had come in, even if a little more slowly than usual. Winty was overtired so he was having a hard job to get to sleep, as he lay there remembering he thought of droving sheep and lambs, pigs and cows with Shep it was all so wonderful? Dad had promised that soon he was going to be allowed to ride on one of the horses, gosh that would be good those horses were so big. Later when he got older he was going to be taught to drive one of the tractors, he had hopes he could drive it with a hay turner that machine that spun the hay for drying that's what the learner farmers do when they start? Meantime the horses were there only to pull the sledge which was used for transport, anywhere on the farm the workers wanted to go to pick up or deliver heavy loads.

Finally Winty drifted off to sleep and immediately started to dream, but it was so real and all mixed up that he started to toss and turn in his distress. First he was dreaming of the pigs, but they were the great big mother pigs, they were not dancing they were looking at Winty and gnashing there great big fangs at him. They would rush at him and Shep ran away leaving Winty by himself, those big pigs kept coming at him their great big mouths wide open and going snap, snap as they opened and shut.

Then just as the pigs reached Winty they turned out to be Lambs running around and jumping, higher than even higher, but the pigs had gone and Shep was back. Then some lambs jumped so high they jumped right over the moon, crikey what a jump then some of the mothers started jumping and they also jumped over the moon? Then all of a sudden Shep jumped over the moon as well it was all so funny, that Winty was thinking maybe I can jump over the moon as well.

All of a sudden the dancing pigs were back but one had a guitar and was playing it using its front toes, gosh thought Winty that's even harder than jumping over the moon. The pigs all stood up on their back feet and started to dance with each other, just like Mum and Dad did when there were parties at home. Suddenly Shep was standing on his hind feet and dancing cheek to cheek with a lady pig, and Winty was playing drums and singing into a microphone, it was a great party. Then Mum and Dad came in and both were throwing pig grits around, but the pigs wouldn't eat the grits they started to talk and they wanted another beer please Mr. or else we are going home? Mum went out and came back with lots of beer for all, she handed it all out and the pigs all started to cheer for her. Dad stepped up and announced he was going to bring the musical implements which ones could play what, all the pigs jumped up and cheered we all can they chorused in delight? Shep was talking too and telling his lady pig he loved her, and would she like to go for a walk.

Suddenly the cow that had shit all over Winty, came in and started to dance with the bull, which had come with her they were both standing on their hind legs and doing the pig dance? After a while all the tiny pigs came in with the great big fierce pigs again, and they started to dance, so the big pigs danced too it was just a grand party for everyone. Every animal at the party was doing the pig dance, round and round oink, oink, moo, moo, baa, baa, but Shep had gone for a walk with the lady pig.

Then there was a full orchestra with all the pigs that had gone to market playing and one of the giant Momma Pigs stepped up and started to sing, but her big fangs were still there and she looked so fierce, Winty got a fright.

Finally the two horses came in still with the sledge behind them, and they started running round the dancers so fast they were nearly beating every one with the sledge.

Suddenly the cow that shits, started to spray everyone and thing with turnip shit, it just sprayed over the whole lot of the dancers. Round and round she went the faster she went the more she sprayed turnip shit. Suddenly the shit turned from shit to turnips, and all of the pigs rushed around eating turnips. The bull started to growl, you silly old shit bag he said, how can you do this there are turnips everywhere and I don't like turnips, you are just a silly old shit bag, we better go home?

Then Winty decided he could jump over the moon and whoosh he did, up he jumped and then he was over the moon, but he stopped for a bite of cheese. Did you know he asked his Dad that the moon is made of cheddar cheese, I had a bite and it was real nice? When he landed he thought gosh maybe I should jump for more cheese, so he did. When he landed back after the second jump the party was over and only Shep was left looking very pleased with himself.

Winty was tossing and turning in his sleep going oink, oink, moo, moo, baa, baas. Suddenly his Mum was shaking him to wake up, are you alright son she asked him. Yes I am fine Mum he smiled it was just a great party, thank you for coming, and the beer was nice the pigs thought you and Dad were grand, and please tell Dad the music was great?

But that Lady Pig she was so ugly with her big teeth, we won't invite her next time.

Haymaking

1942: #12

There that time of the year that in all farming communities is special, and that's haymaking a time when all gather together at that golden time of the year. And so it has been for millennia and will be in the years ahead, that rare period of human unity.

Winty had been out riding on the tractor while the grass for hay was being cut, they were up in the high country, and had to cut around eighty Hectares. After the initial excitement it was all rather boring, just going round and round jumping down every now and again to clear the cutters when they blocked up? Winty had discovered long ago the tractor was boring, gosh his Dad must be tough, and he had to sit on a tractor between milking so very often. Ploughing, (digging the soil) seeding, (planting new seeds) harrowing, (raking the paddocks to spread the manure after the cows have been in) there was just so many jobs round the farm, that needed one of the tractors.

When his Mum and Dad started talking about hay and silage (green un dried hay) making, he had got so excited, then when he saw Dad setting up the cutters to attach to a tractor, he had been disappointed. Dad was pleased Winty did not like the tractor; just imagine he had thought having to answer questions all day, while he was trying to cut straight rows impossible? But haymaking was different, it was like shearing, the surrounding farmers all worked together to harvest the crop.

They had different machines, the cutters were just an attachment to any tractor, and the tedding (a type of rake) machine turned the hay over after

117

it was cut so it could dry. The baler was a big machine owned by a contract farmer, this great big machine gathered up the hay as it passed by, then cut and formed the bales it also secured the bales with either twine or wire? The stacker to lift the hay onto trucks then off again into hay barns, this was only done by farmers who wanted to keep the hay to feed out to the herd? Some of the farmers who had very fertile soil, sold their hay and silage to others with less productive soil, and poor grass growth.

It was normal for the farmers to own different machines, and to work together to bring in the crops, and the Wives' and Daughters would bring meals so the men could keep working all day. The Baler was charged for by the hour not by the bale, so the quicker they got rid of him the better! That first year Winty had not known haymaking was an almost festive affair, as the men worked and the women bought food and drink, everybody loved haymaking time. They were all young families, so there were a lot of boys and girls to play with, most of them were small like Winty, and he knew them from school? All of the bigger children would be working, doing small jobs round the farms, normally done by their parent's, as soon as they got home from school?

Babies would be looked after by one of the mothers at her home, they all took turns at that job because all wanted to be out in the paddocks. After all of the hay is in and all the work is done, it is normal to have the Haymaking Ball, everybody celebrates it means they have beaten the rain and the crop is safe for another year. The hay must be dry before it can be baled or else it may burn and never dry, the cows will not eat such spoiled hay.

Winty and Shep spent the time frolicking around the bare paddock, and really enjoyed themselves, no animals just the two of them playing.

On the day it was Mum's turn to mind the children, there was no one to keep an eye on what Winty was up to. It was time for the lunch break and the machines had all stopped, it was quiet when all of a sudden a tremendous noise broke out. Winty had been playing in one of the trucks, and had without knowing what he was doing, had let the brakes get released.

The truck had only been secured with the brakes and it was on a slope, so as soon as the brakes were released it started to roll down the hill? Winty was so scared he did not know what to do, all he could do was sit and yell for his Dad, who of course couldn't hear his Son.

Down the hill that old truck rolled, then suddenly right in front was that great big baler, with the trailer for catching the bales attached. Shep was running around outside and trying to attract attention, but no one either heard or understood he was ignored!

Boom the truck collided into the trailer and Winty went flying into the windscreen of the truck, there was no real damage to either the trailer or the truck just Winty. Winty was knocked unconscious, and by the time the men got to the truck, blood was coming out of his mouth. When Dad got to him he had slumped back onto the truck seat, and was laying there with his eyes shut and not moving?

The men were petrified, one ran for his car that was close by, and Dad, who was shaking with fright, picked up Winty in his arms and ran to that car. The man who owned the truck was over whelmed, he knew he was in the wrong, leaving the truck on a slight incline, and not in gear was a serious mistake. Winty should not have been in the truck that was true, but he was only six YOA and had not been properly looked after, that was the real problem?

It was a twenty minute drive to the Hospital, and the old car rattled along with the driver driving as fast as it would travel. Someone else had gone to warn Mum, and another Mum had gone to get the children, she had been taking care of.

By the time Winty's Mum got to the Hospital he was in the operating room! Of course the two parents were frantic, then the word came through it was a serious Cerebral Edema! Winty had to be flown to Auckland Hospital, because their local Hospital was not well enough quipped for such an operation, and had no Surgeon close by even if it had been?

A helicopter service had only months before been put in service, and Winty and his parents were to be picked up within fifteen minutes. By the time the transport arrived Winty had been prepared for the operation in Auckland, and he with his parents were rushed on board the Helicopter straight away?

Learning to Swim

Jan 1941: #13

We all love to swim, especially in NZ an Island Country, but can we learn as quickly as my pet dog did? Yes we can because my Dad is a great teacher you'll see, said the little boy in anger?

Crikey Mum the Teacher told us today we all had to learn how to swim, there is a big pool at the school and we are going to have lessons? Winty had come home from school very excited, normally he hated school, but this was different he wanted to learn to swim. Sadly it was not to be because the family was soon to leave the area and shift to a farm in Titirangi just north of Auckland. The shift would be within the next month, which meant there may not be time for many swimming lessons. Mum gave Winty a big hug and told him that maybe there would be a swimming pool at his new school? Winty had started in the tiny tot's school, he was now five years and four months old! He had a letter from school for his Mother to sign, giving permission for the lessons which would start the next day, and continue once weekly for the rest of the term!

The next day Winty was up early and ready to leave for school at 6.00am, but school did not start until 9.00am so he had a long wait. Finally it was time to leave home he had his school bag packed, with his reading and arithmetic book, lunch and his swim trunks and towel. Winty was so excited, he was running around with his pet dog, and telling the dog just what a great day it was, he, Winty was going swimming just like his dog could swim?

At 8.45 he was allowed to leave home and within ten minutes he was at school and waiting for the school bell to ring signaling starting time. Running up to the Teacher Winty asked, what time do we go swimming, we are ready to go swimming now please. Winty had been told that when he asked for anything he must say please, and if he did he would be allowed to do whatever it was he wanted, his Parents had made a big mistake?

No Winty you cannot go swimming until after dinnertime then it is our turn, but we cannot go now, it's not our turn yet. No I just said please so that means we must go now, said an angry Winty didn't you hear me, let me say it again can we go swimming now please, 'teacher'?

Winty there is nothing I can do it's not our turn, we cannot go now until after dinner then I will take you. No that's not right if you tell me to do something you never say please you just tell me to do this or do that. I am doing the right thing, my Mummy has told me that if we say please, then what we are asking for we will get. You are not being fair teacher and I want to go home, I don't want to go swimming anymore. This school is no good and you are not fair teacher, my Mummy said I had to say please, I have done that twice and still you are saying no. I want to go home now please, I don't like you anymore?

Poor Teacher, she didn't know what to say, Winty was an intelligent child and it was true she had made a mistake; in not telling the children what time the swimming was to start? She had also failed to say the lesson was only for one hour, Winty had obviously thought he was going swimming all day, what could she do? Winty was the easiest pupil to teach and yet the hardest, if ever a mistake was made he was sure to pick it up, and follow thru, if it was something he wanted. If he didn't want what had been said then he would forget it, this child she was thinking, has a very selective memory. Looking at Winty she said, I need to check out to see if the schedule can be changed, class will all wait here please, I will be back soon.

When she returned she had a big smile for the whole class and said, we are going to have an extra lesson at the same time as the class that is going in now. Children will all please change into your swimming costume; and we will go straight to the pool, the lesson is for an hour. Because it was my mistake the Principle has allowed us to have two swimming periods today, all children should thank you Winty! Winty will you please take a note from me to your Mummy today when you go home?

After school Winty went straight home with the note and gave it to his Mum for her to read.

Mrs. Stephens the Teacher had written: Today Winty has had a big day, I made a mistake and never said please, at a point where I should have said it. This has meant that two changes had to be made to the school's curriculum today. Sadly Winty has left school with an even bigger question of results when saying.

He tells me his dog got into some deep water and he asked his Daddy, to please make sure his dog could swim and he did? Apparently the dog swam because Winty said please. Today Winty said to our swimming teacher, please Sir Will you make sure I will be able to swim today, but of course he couldn't achieve that goal all in one day.

Winty was so upset he now thinks we teachers don't listen when he says please, he wants his Daddy to please teach him how to swim, the same way as he taught his dog to swim. Winty trusts his Dad, but also he has seen the dog swim because of his Dad. You need to have a good talk with Winty to explain that please only works when used properly, not just when he wants something?

If this isn't done you his Dad and we Teachers are in for a very hard time, now and in the future, sincerely please!

Stolen peaches

1947: #14

Stolen fruit just seems natural for boys of all ages, they seem to look and taste better than the ones in the orchid at home. Ask any boy he will agree yes that is true?

The paper boy couldn't believe his eyes were those peaches real? They were so big and juicy but there was only four of them. Even as he looked he thought, "Yes the trees at home would be in full fruit, but none would have alluring peaches of such size and color," no trees he knew of could match these amazing fruit. It had been a hard morning, one of the other boys was off work sick, and Vincent had been asked to do a double run. Vincent lived in Freeman's Bay with his Auntie Clare; and was renowned for his work ethic. Every morning at 4.00am he rode his bicycle from 'Freeman's Bay to the Herne Bay High School, to pick up his 200 New Zealand Heralds'; and deliver to the customers. The Vendor had asked Vincent to do the extra run up College Hill, and down Ponsonby Rd a big double run, but the Vendor knew Vince could do the job.

The peach tree was on the extra run Vincent was delivering too. There at a customer's little house half way up College Hill; was a solitary peach tree planted in the middle of the front lawn. Those peaches in all their glory, four magnificent fruit seemed to be saying to Vincent take us we are all yours! Vince was transfixed, how he wandered could such peaches be growing on a spindly little tree in the middle of the city, it didn't make sense?

The house owners were surely silly; didn't they know they would be irresistible to paper boys, especially farm boys? With a sad sigh Vincent decided he wouldn't take the peaches, after all there were many peaches on the trees back home in Avondale, and on the farm in Titirangi, but oh my none of the home peaches could match these four! That day when he got home after school, Aunt Claire told Vincent the Vendor had been around and told her he needed to have him do the extra run for a week, because the other boy was still off sick.

And so it was for that whole week, Vincent delivered the papers to that house, and had to look at those four beautiful peaches it just wasn't fair. Why he wandered didn't the owners of that tree pick their peaches they were ripe, and needed to be picked else the birds would steal them. On the last day Vince had to do that run he could restrain himself no longer, he decided it was either him or the birds, the owners had no right anymore cos they were leaving fruit, that were now becoming over ripe and wasted. Anyhow it was but a minute and those four peaches were sitting in Vince's paper delivery bag, they had just been rescued from those awful greedy birds and uncaring owners.

Vince got home with those peaches, but suddenly he was guilt stricken, what if he hadn't saved the peaches from the birds at all. What if that little old home was owned by old people who just hadn't had time to pick those four beautiful peaches, oh dear such a guilty conscience, he just couldn't eat those damned peaches.

Vincent decided he would hide the fruit in one of the drawers at home while he considered what he must do with them. The next morning it was still the same, he still felt guilty over those peaches oh my what to do. He decided to confide in his Aunt Claire what he had done, and how he was undecided whether to eat them or take them back to that little house, and confess his theft.

Clare was indignant, "of course you must take them back," she said, that's stealing," I will tell Mum on you, "what a nasty little boy you are."

Suitably chastised Vince was one very sorry boy at school that day, he had disgraced himself and now Claire was going to tell Mum, woe is me what a nasty fellow, he had turned out to be a disgrace to the Stephens family. All day Vince pondered how he could have done such a dreadful thing, oh if only he could take his actions all back, what would Mum say would Aunt Claire tell her today?

Vince didn't go straight home from school that day, he was too ashamed his beloved Aunt was ashamed of him, and Mum was probably waiting with her broom, but this time she would be really angry. Well there was no choice it was time to face the music, so he snuck home and slipped quietly in the door then waited for the explosion. That's funny there was no comments or accusations of thief. Mum was contentedly playing cards by herself, and greeted Vince with a smile and a big kiss, Aunt Claire was such a beam of light with a big smile and no accusing looks?

Vince couldn't believe his luck; he decided he would take those peaches back to the little house immediately, while his luck was still in.

Going to the cupboard he opened the drawer that had the peaches in, but lo and behold no peaches, what had happened had Aunt Claire returned them? No she couldn't do that because she didn't know where the house was. Oh well no way around it he would have to ask Aunt Claire where the peaches were, bound to be more problems, but never mind better get it over and done with?

"Aunt Claire where are those peaches," Vincent asked quietly so Mum didn't hear.

'Oh we ate them for dinner today, Mum wanted to know where you had got such beautiful peaches.'

"What" Vince wailed indignantly, "You told me I was a nasty little thief this morning!" "Yes so I decided to save you and eat the stolen peaches thank me for saving you; you were a nasty little boy this morning you aren't now."

Marble Champion

1944: #15

The winner is always the best, except when its two boys trying to beat each other, the maybe really the loser is sometimes the best?

The game had been going on for a while and Winty was winning as usual, but the loser was getting upset. In 1944 marbles couldn't be bought in the shops, not even at Woolworths' so Winty had introduced a form of gambling. Winner takes all but Winty always won, then he sold the marbles back for three pence each. He had also found a source of fabulous marbles from an eighteen year old girl, who had bought two hundred of them before Woolies stopped selling them. She was now an adult and by the look of the marbles, she hadn't played with them anyhow. Winty had bought the lot of her for two pence each and was selling them as well as winning them back. These were top class marbles, and Winty was selling them for six pence each because they were superior colors and had no cracks, see they are as good as new they have never been played with.

Billy Farrow and Winty was both nine YOA, and had been playing for about three hours and Winty was winning by a big margin. Billy was getting upset, but Winty was just keeping the pressure on. Billy had bought fifty marbles off Winty at six pence each, but Winty had now won over half of them back.

It had been a good day for Winty he had bought two hundred marbles for two pence each and had already sold one hundred at six pence each. The problem was he had already won seventy of them back off several of his customers, but Billy was the biggest loser. Now the problem was what price Billy could buy his marbles back? Winty allowed they were now used, but still wanted four pence for the ones he had sold first at six pence. Billy wanted to pay only three pence because Winty had already got six pence each off him, and always sold his used marbles for three pence each, so why had he put his price up?

After all only the ones we have played with were now used, and that was only two of them the rest were still new, so Winty had said OK Billy let's play some more maybe you will win them back and that will make you happy, but don't forget if I win you will be further in hock for more marbles. So the game was continued with first Winty letting Billy win and then they had another break when Billy had won fifteen back now he was only down ten and he was really happy.

Suddenly Winty said look I am getting tired let's play again after and you can win your losses back then, OK? No said Billy you are still winning and I want to get all of mine back, we have to keep playing. OK said Winty secretly giggling to himself I am very tired, but you are the one who is setting the rules let's play and no whinging if you lose. No said Billy, but don't you whine when I win and take your marbles as well as the ones you had won off me.

Oh that's no problem my belief is if you win it means you are the better player, so it's only fair for you to get all of my marbles.

The game started again and before long Winty had won thirty five marbles off Billy which left him with only five left. Do you want to keep playing or can we leave it until later, I am happy to play you anytime so you can get your marbles back?

Poor Billy he was a bit dumb as Winty well knew, and his parents spoiled him by giving him lots of pocket money, that's why he was being set up to lose the lot and have to buy more. Winty had already got one pound five shillings of him, but knew he could get more money, whatever he wanted, this was a prime sucker.

OK says Winty your luck may change, but there's no doubt my lucks in so far today. Crikey the games too hot for Billy, his luck has just completely run out and now Winty has won the rest of the fifty, Billy had at first bought off him. Crikey Billy he said it's not your lucky day, but it is mine just as well you made me play you some, more now I have all the marbles again.

Yeah said poor dumb Billy you're lucky today all right, but now I have no more marbles to play so how much to buy my fifty back?

Look you can get the whole lot back for one pound, but because I was so lucky let's say you pay me eighteen shillings that's very fair now Billy. I can sell those marbles to someone else for sixpence each you know that don't you?

Then the argument started Billy only wanted to pay fifteen shillings on the basis he was buying his marbles back, and Winty refused less than eighteen shillings. The argument was getting intense, but at that stage no fighting was even thought about.

You fight him Winty don't be a coward fight him, or else I will come and give you a hiding myself.

Billy was so pleased he could see himself getting his marbles back just for giving Winty a hiding, he was far bigger and thought he could win easily.

Ok Winty yelled at Claire shut up will ya yeah if you insist its s fight, but it's just stupid?

'You fight him squawked Claire or else'.

So the fight was on, but unfortunately for Billy he got the hiding not Winty, so as he ran away home he threw a big stone at Claire, from whom she had yelled take that now white boy.

Now see she said to Winty that's what you should have done from the start, don't play silly games with those kids stick up for yourself!

Sure said Winty and you will send me broke, I was close to getting another eighteen shillings of that mug. Yeah thanks a lot genius it's a lesson for me to remember, not to argue about money in front of you thanks Clare, you sure are smart orright a bloody genius!

My kid can ride a horse

1946: #16

Some of these Pakehas' are real smart others are real stupid, just ask Vincent. These two were real stupid!

The Aran St Avondale riding school Saturday morning, and the horses were all curry combed, and saddled up ready to work and Vincent was all decked out in his teaching togs. Percy Browne was adamant Vincent was a champion rider, and he was going to be an equally good teacher. The horses cost three shillings and sixpence per hour for the hire and another five shillings per hour if Vincent's teaching was required. (Price included a horse for Vincent) There were twenty horses in work at the school, 'of varying temperament and all beautiful animals'. Most were retired racehorses bought at auction by Percy, all kept shod and checked daily by him, when they were working.

Any how it was riding school time and Vincent was fondling one of the horses, when a big luxury car pulled up and a Youth and his Mum got out. The Youth was dressed in immaculate riding gear, very expensive and his Mother showed all the indications of an eccentric old cow, which she was! Vincent was horrified he knew what was coming, he had been teaching this Youth for several weeks, and now the Mother was convinced her son was an expert rider. In fact the kid was hopeless, and would never be able to sit a horse properly.

The Kid had on riding boots and fancy cowboy gear, a strict rule at the school was no sharpened spurs were allowed, actually not even blunted ones. But here came this foolish Mother and her arrogant Son, strutting over

129

towards the horses, the Son outfitted with a full set of Mexican spurs, with real cruel cutters fully sharpened.

"Those spurs cannot be used on our horses," protested Vince, "they are very sharp and cruel our horses are not used to such barbaric riding you will tear their flanks? Even experienced riders damage the flanks, and you are just a learner."

"Listen to me you little nothing," sneered the Mother, "my Son will ride with that gear on and he will teach you just what a real rider he is. For us you aren't necessary anymore, you are just an incompetent little Maori nothing don't tell us what we can or cannot do."

"Ok as you wish '" replied Vince, "But be warned these horses won't respond well to those spurs."

'Pepper was saddled up and the Youth with his fancy spurs was legged up to that big fractious gelding, Vince knew Pepper and he knew what was going to happen the minute Pepper got the first taste of those vicious spurs'.

The Kid with a whoop of delight and silly bravado immediately raked Pepper full cut with his spurs. Pepper let out an angry squeal, pig rooted on the spot and took off at full gallop, the Kid yelling in delight.

At the back of the farm there was a forest of gorse mostly up to twelve feet in height, but all of the horses had their saddle high tunnels; into which they used to go to avoid the sun. With a rider on top there was no way that rider could avoid the gorse thorns, and if he didn't he would be badly ripped.

'Pepper was of for that thorn patch the Kid yelling; and his mother screaming her delight and encouragement'.

'I told you Maori Boy, she yelled my Son can do anything'.

'Suddenly there was a scream of pain from her Son as the horse reached the gorse bushes, and without even slowing down lowered its head and ran straight in'.

The Son managed to get thrown off the horse, but only after being badly scratched. Pepper was nowhere to be seen he wasn't coming back for that sort of treatment.

'Both Mother and Son were screaming, the Son in pain the Mother in anger'.

"I warned you," said Vince, "our horses can't be ridden with any sort of spurs but you wouldn't listen."

"You have deliberately mislead us," screamed the old Mum, "my Son will punish you just as soon as he gets over his pain you just wait and see!"

Vincent's always volatile temper sprang to the surface, "Punish me he laughed, your silly idiot Son is a coward, anyone that would do what he did to our horse is a coward. Bring him back when he is recovered and I will beat his silly butt for him, I am not a horse and will fix him real quick. As for you, how can he be anything but an idiot, he looks like you, he sounds like you and he thinks like a Pakeha, just like you, now what have you got to say to this little Maori nothing now. Say the wrong thing and I will beat his silly butt right now. Oh by the way I box and lift weights, lets meet at the gym anytime you like, that white coon's older than me but he's just another White Fella; so that's not a problem.

Just then Percy came out of the house and asked, "what's all of the noise about?"

"This little Maori basted has hurt my Son," screamed Mum.

"I warned them," protested Vincent, "they insisted on those spurs he has on and Pepper took off into the bushes as soon as his flanks were raked,"

"That Maori did this on purpose," screamed both Mother and Son, Percy's face started to go red as soon as he got a full look at the spurs. "That's my Son," he screamed, "and I am going to sue you if you have ripped my horse's flanks, that's an expensive animal.

Oh, you will be hearing from the RSPC as well, those Mexican spurs sharpened like that are illegal. Now get of this property and never come back; I have your car number so we will be coming for you?"

A top Caddy

Sadly some have all of the advantages yet never learn this bloody game, Winty was one of those!

Titirangi Golf Course back when this was the top course in the country, Winty was one of the top Caddy's; this meant he only caddied for low handicap players? 'In Golf Jargon any player above a seven handicap was then a hacker, and only for low grade Caddy's to work for'! Usually a top Caddy would stick to one player, in Vince's case his player was the Australasian Champion in 1939 and played off a plus one handicap? Titirangi was a par 74 so his handicap was set to 73 for the course ie; if he was playing someone on a 4 handicap he had to give his opponent 5 strokes start over the full 18 holes in a round.

Another advantage of working for a good player meant the caddy was able to learn, watching his man play. There was only one player on a lower handicap than the player Vince worked for; he was on a plus two handicap? It was usual to work every week end and usually that meant two rounds on Saturday, and another two on Sunday! It has been difficult to understand why the rounds played now are so slow! We believe it must be that now the average handicap is far higher, and that means slower play as far more shots are played. When Winty was a Caddy Golf was a game for the wealthy, thankfully now it's a game for everyone, and all ages. For Winty watching family members play; it is amusing how the rules are interpreted, some of the comments made about rules during play can only be called hilarious.

The great Sth African Bobby Locke came to Titirangi for an exhibition match in 1945 and Winty then a junior Caddy, was delighted to watch that great man play. Bobby Locke had a rather rotund physique a little over weight. A great player to watch his short game was a pleasure to see, but his long woods and irons were good as well. Overall he was one of the world greats of his time, and Winty took it as a privilege to see him play. Accredited Caddies were allowed to watch these International events free of charge, but paid the green fee of three pence.

The only other great player Winty had the luck to watch was Norman Von Nida, who played an exhibition against New Zealand's Alex Murray, an ex winner of the NZ Professional Championship. Von Nida was a small compact man who when he opened up with a drive, the distance achieved belied his size. Alex Murray was a top player, but that day was totally outclassed by the Von as Von Nida was known? Winty was the Caddy for Alex Murray, and Jack Oliver then the head caddy at Titirangi Caddied for the Von. Winty was by then one of the clubs top Caddy's and was selected on seniority to Caddy for Alex Murray.

At the first a par four about three hundred and eighty yards the Von had a drive and eighty yard pitch into the green for an easy par. The par five fifth with a lengthy of 520 yards with no wind it was a drive and a seven iron for the Von, and a birdie four. The sixth a dogleg to the left was about four hundred and fifty yards long, but with a good drive to a flat plateau the green was easy to reach with a drive and pitch shot? It was an easy par five, and was classified the easiest hole on the course.

Trying to decide where he should place his drive, the Von scrambled up a tree on the back of the tee to check where his drive should be placed. If anyone had taken a photo it would have been quite valuable. Having seen the necessary place, he took out a three wood and placed the ball exactly where it would be best for a high shot into the green? It was a spectacular play and loudly applauded by all of the spectators a birdie four! The seventh is a par three over a ravine two hundred and ten yards and the green had three levels. The Von played a six iron and spun the ball back to ten feet from the hole for a birdie two.

The eighth three hundred and forty yards the Von nearly drove the green, a running shot and one put for another birdie. The ninth another par four at three hundred and eighty yards was another easy hole, but a missed put meant he only got another par! He turned in thirty three while Alex Murray turned in thirty five still a good score, but poor compared to the Von.

The second nine holes the Von played the tenth in a par four, and very easy. The eleventh a par three was again a birdie two. The twelfth another par four was a drive and pitch for another par four. The thirteenth the hardest hole on the course was made to look simple with a Birdie three. The seventeenth he had another Birdie and the eighteenth similarly made easy for another par. Von Nida played the second nine holes in thirty three for a full round of sixty six, eight under the card. Winty's player Alex Murray played another half of thirty five for a very respectable seventy, and four under the card, but still lost by four strokes how frustrating can the game be?

This was the highlight of Vince's Golf Caddy career; he tried to play but could never get better than a ten handicap, even though the Caddies received free lessons from club pro. He was never good enough, so he gave the game up. There are enough hackers out there now without Vince digging up the course and losing balls! Ironically he was sponsored to join the Titirangi course as a member, he would have been the first Maori member of that club, had he accepted?

The Rodeo

1950: #18

Ride em and smile, there's them that can and that there's them that cant, and there's them that's both Winty, was one of the both!

The rodeo was coming to town and it was exciting, they had a horse the Widow maker a big black ugly Stallion, in the show. He was reputed to be the worst and most dangerous horse, ever to try and ride? The prize offered was one hundred pounds for staying on for ten seconds! Nobody had told Winty's family the rodeo was in town, and he was sure, he thought to win the one hundred quid prize, he hoped he could keep it all for himself? If the family had known his Stepfather would be there equally sure Winty would win, and would take the prize for himself.

Several of Winty's friends would try, but Winty knew they would have no chance! Ever since he had first been hoisted onto the back of a horse Winty had been a natural horseman, (boy) he had found it very easy to sit a horse bucking or not.

The family used to own and operate a riding school, and Winty had been teaching riding for about two years from 13 YOA! He also rode track work at the Avondale race track in the mornings, and earned ten shillings for the four hours work. Some of the horses had been broken in (Trained) for riding the old fashioned way, by Winty, saddle em up cowboy and ride em till they drop or you do? This was different than a Rodeo where there could be spikes under the saddle, to drive a crazy horse even crazier. The prize was never easily won, there was always some tricks used; to make sure it was a hard ride, Winty knew that but didn't care?

Maoris' like the Australian Aboriginals are natural horsemen, but the tricks used at rodeos' are not usually known by the average rider? Once an Aboriginal or Maori gets up on a horse they are very hard to dislodge, the old saying is they stick like shit to a blanket! They don't need saddles and even with a flank rope (Lasso around the horse's flanks) are hard to dislodge! If the flank rope is left on the horse will lash out with its hooves and will circle the ring lashing out! The whites are often good too, but when they are they are far more professional in approach, therefore better.

Winty had no horses at home to train with, and even if there had been one to break in, he would not have wanted anyone at home to know, what he was up too. 'The riding school was very busy, but he was only teaching learners, and they were only ever put up on the really docile animals' anyhow! Very few learners were naturals on a horse, usually they had indulgent parents, who were catering to their children's every whim's not skills? To be a teacher Winty had to listen to all of the Parents whinging about the prices and their children, complaining because the horse were too big or something equally silly. Winty had no patience for teaching yet oddly was well liked usually by both learners and their parents, not that he really cared. He didn't get paid for his work anyhow, and at this time was feeling rebellious toward his Stepfather! Why he wandered should I have to work and get nothing for it, its lousy being broke all of the time? His Stepfather took all of the earning and Winty got nothing for his work.

The big day was here, it was on a Friday night and the crowd was big and noisy! 'Winty stood back to let the others ride first knowing none were good enough, but would help to tire the horse? Sure enough he was right none went anymore than a few seconds', but the horse showed no signs of getting tired! He was a big vicious brute at least seventeen hands high, with crazy eyes and he was a bite-er as well! The rider had to keep a firm grip on the horse's reins because if let loose he would bite very hard! This horse was really crazy, and did not care how all he wanted to do was to if he could, kill the rider who was on his back. This was probably due to a spike in the saddle!

Vince was up and the horses flank rope had been released it was all go, that crazy brute first took off with four feet at once off the ground, and it's bank arched. That move was easy it would take far more than that to drop Winty. The next was as if the horse had become a snake, as the front end seemed to separate from the rear end, and it shimmied round the ring also easy for Winty to beat? The ride was almost up with the prize in sight suddenly, it was as if the Horse was going to roll over onto the saddle on the ground! This was an unexpected and dangerous move; it was an attempt by the horse to crush the rider? Winty actually jumped off and it was only at nine seconds so the ride was lost.

How disappointing beaten by that crazy brute, but hey why not go again? So swapping shirts with a friend for a disguise he was ready to go again! The horse was back in the shoot and the crowd was screaming for more, Winty was mounted for his second try? Suddenly the loudspeaker announced this rider was up last time no second rides, get off that horse Son. The crowd went crazy with their 'Boos etc'; but management was adamant no second ride for this man. It was only a fluke their horse had beaten this rider a few minutes ago, and he was not to go again? One hundred quid was a lot of money, and not given away easily.

What a disappointment Winty went home with empty pockets, the same way he had arrived broke, hungry and thirsty._

The Bull and the electric fence

1957: #19

Ever thought of what it would be like to put your doodle on an electric fence on full bull charge, NO? Well let me tell ya about a big Friesian Bull that accidentally did!

Good morning Mate how are you feeling? We have two Jersey cows coming into season; (Mating) and you need to make sure that damned Friesian Bull doesn't get at them before milking time tonight; they have to go to the Jersey Bull. 'Just to be safe put the electric fence on full bull strength so that big fella can't get at them cows, he can be real dangerous when he knows there are cows ready and he can't get to them'. The cows are in the next paddock but they should be right, find yourself some work to do where you can keep an eye on them.

OK Boss there is some fences to be mended in that paddock so I will do that today, and at the same time keep an eye on the big bloke. He doesn't like us anyhow he blames me when he misses out and the little Jersey gets a go, pity there wasn't one for each of them. The fences stop the Jersey Bull but that big Friesian if he sees cows on heat that's it, he just goes straight through doesn't even feel the barbed wire, but the electric fence usually stops him.

Now down next to the Bull paddock: Good morning Bully Boy how is your mood today? Don't blame me if the cows come in and you miss out, you just aint the right breed for this lot. Anyhow the boss says there is two of the girls' coming into season today so I guess you're going to be real annoyed with me. Never mind the fence is on full strength for you big fella so you had better behave. All of a sudden there's a low growl from Bully boy he is very agitated the boss was right two of the cows are in heat and showing up strong. 'They are jumping on each other's backs and playing at being Lesbians and boy is Bully Boy getting annoyed, he is looking at me and wishing he could kick my butt'.

Wow there he goes he just touched the electricity, boy look at him jump. Now he is pacing up and down that wire and looking at me as if to say, "Mate if only I could get a hold of you it would be a great pleasure to stamp you into the ground; before going down to look after those two females."

'Wow look at those cows boy they sure are hot for the bull sorry about that, but orders are orders and they aint for you fella the little fella gets both of them at milking time'. Look at Jersey Joe way over in those top paddocks, 'he doesn't even know he's got such a nice present tonight if he did he would be kicking up a fuss and wanting them now'.

'Up and down up and down Bully Boy stamps in anger, all the time looking at me in a terrible rage. If looks could kill I would have been dead over an hour ago'.

If he did get through the electric and barbed wire fence there is no way anyone could stop him except those two cows down there in the herd. 'Those females are still going crazy it's as if they are deliberately teasing Bully Boy', but hell they are only cows surely they aint doing that to the poor bugger or are they? 'Crikey look at that he's has his old doodle unsheathed and its hanging down eighteen inches' and swinging from side to side as he walks up and down those wire and electric fences.

Crikey look at those females down there trying to ride the rest of the herd, go for it girls make the big boy swing it higher, he is getting madder and madder by the minute.

Crikey look whats happening now, the entire herd (100 cows) are coming up to the dividing fence to see what bully is going crook about. 'They are standing there over the fence all are shaking their heads as if to say whats wrong with you, you big oaf'? The old cows seem to be saying serves you right, we have to listen to you growling every day!

Wow that was close he nearly hit the electric fence that time, wander what it would be like to get a full shot out of that fence, crikey it would hurt for sure, careful old fella if you aint careful you sure are going to get a shock in your britches, that you won't forget in a hurry?

'Wow there's a go that was less than an inch from the wire; listen to the Big Fella growl, but that aint nothing to what he will have to say if he just swings that thing a little higher'.

Oh now this is tough stuff those two that are in season are right up next to him and still playing around with each other. 'They are really turning on an act for him and the herd I suppose, damned cows they are sillier than ever today'.

'Look at him go and listen to that roar no it's a real bellow now, boy is he mad. He's pacing up and down and looking at me with such anger in his bully eyes, if he could get a hold of me I can see that wish in his eyes'.

'Oh my goodness that done it he hit the electric fence with his doodle, now look at him go his poor old doodle has gone purple, and he is rushing around now as if the world fell on him maybe it'?

'Poor old Bully Boy, he has stopped growling and is trying to fit his massive head under his chest to lick his poor old cooked doodle. His doodle, well that's gone all blue now, wonder if it will still work? Oh well the shows over guess I better get on with this fencing now, but for sure there will be no work done by me in Bully Boys paddock today'!

Meat from Work

Auckland NZ, 1950: #20

Crikey boss that's not stealing everyone gets free meat here just watch them? And if it's good for enough for them, why not me too?

Winty had got just his first job it was Oct 26 1950, he had left Seddon Memorial Tech College on the day he turned fifteen years of age, and had gone out to the Southdown export meat works the next day for a job. He had always wanted to be like his hero Uncle George Kipa, Aunt Claire's husband, now he was going to be an expert to. Winty had been told by several of his Uncle's friends just how much of an expert his Uncle was; and he admired any expert who had made it with personal skill. Winty was an orphan and he had been living with various family members for a long time! But by his own choice he lived mainly with Aunt Claire and Uncle George. He was a very independent youngster, but George was his hero and that was because his Nana Mary had told him what a good man his Uncle was, so he wanted to be the same. Winty had always been very quick mentally, and it didn't take him more than a couple of days to think that meat was free; because he could see so many of the workers helping themselves, during the lunch break.

It was quite amazing because Winty did have skills that were needed to get to his goal, which was to copy his Uncle, 'within two months he was learning rapidly'. The foreman had gone out of his way to teach Winty because he knew Uncle George and he liked Winty, because he had shown he was a good worker.

In those years just after WW11 was over, there was over employment, anybody with a good work ethic could get a job at any time. 'Maoris' were very popular in the skilled laboring classes, because they were/are strong and good in certain jobs like Shearing, Slaughtering Beef, Sheep and Pigs, Road Making and Driving' heavy equipment etc; all heavy work. The meat processing industry employed about 75% Maoris' in its contract worker teams, but the unskilled work was about 75% European. The contracts were on average too heavy for Whites'.

The new season was starting on the 10th Dec 1950, Winty was very proud when he was selected to be on the number two team. Being on the number two team meant they would be on full contract within thirty days, this was far better than the learners team. Winty couldn't wait to tell his Uncle and Aunt, that he would be a full contract man at the age of fifteen. This turned out to be true as a member of the number two gang, which would be a full contract team before the 10th January 1951, Aunt Claire was proud of her Nephews efforts.

Back then there was about fifteen different jobs in a full contract team, to be a contractor a man only had to be able to do one, maybe two different jobs. Within three months, Winty could do the full range of different jobs at full contract pace. Having said all these things about his progress as a contract worker, Winty didn't really know much about meat works routine right or wrong, as it was in 1951; all he knew was what he saw the adult men doing? Every day he noticed that at smoko time and lunch time, he could see the men filling up their bags with various cuts of mainly beef. These meats they were cutting off the hanging carcasses and Winty used to watch with growing interest, it seemed the workers got free meat on top of their wages.

This is pretty good thing Winty thought the average wage for workers is about eight pound per week; we are earning twenty five pounds per week. It seems we are getting free meat as well, so I better get my share like the rest of them here. There are plenty of my relations out there that will buy meat off me, and if it's cheap they will buy everything I get that's no problem.

The next day Winty decided he would get his free meat and at the lunch break, started to cut off the, what he guessed were the best beef cuts he could find! Suddenly the foreman who had befriended him came up and said what the hell you think you are doing stealing meat, damn me you are only a kid and stealing already? This isn't stealing all the blokes here get their meat at dinner time, what the hell are you talking about every man here has his free meat, and I bet so do you. That may be so but at least they hide what they are doing, you are just helping yourself even though you knew I was watching you; so you are a bloody thief!

Bull dust if someone hides it from you he is a thief did you see me hiding anything, so who is the bloody thief here it's not me? Go catch all of the thieves; and by the way when you do there will be no staff left here to kill your beef, sheep and pigs so the place will close down, so much for thieves cos you hire them all.

Get down off that ladder so I can kick you up the arse, you cheeky little bugger said the foreman in feigned anger. You have been taught here, you are on top wages even though I bet you are no more than fifteen, and still you steal!

I am not a thief you are just making me a bad guy and I am not so Bugger you too! Sure if you can catch me you can kick my butt as you say, but you are going to have a sore foot cos you will have to kick the butt of every man working here. But listen to me you old bugger, you will never catch me you would be too slow, so there.

The old foremen let out a bellow of laughter, Bugger of out of here he bellowed and next time don't steal when you know I can see you, now again Bugger off.

The champion Shearer

1957: #21

A man is a man and a boy is still just a young man growing up!

It was starting time in the shed and the pens were all full, Vince was working in the next pen to his mate Ray Puke. He had been for the last week telling Puke; and anyone else who would listen, he was the shed 'Gun' (Fastest and cleanest) shearer in the team. Nobody was listening Vince was the youngest in the shed and was considered to be a very smart kid, but a pain in the butt, with his shouts of come on let's do it now, let's go I wanna go home early today? Vince was nearly twenty two YOA and as quick with the shears as he was with a knife, but he was not as strong as the mature men even, if he thought he was stronger! Shearing needs a strong back and quick hands. It also needs unusual strength, Vince might be the quickest over ten sheep, but more than that the older and stronger men would beat him, with their greater endurance.

One day it had to come to a head and it did! Ray Puke came in with a bad mood on, and when Vince started he said, 'all right you noisy little shit, let me show you who the shed gun really is here, and it aint you Buddy'? Ok you yardies fill em up twenty in hot shots pen and twenty in mine. Vince fell for it Puke was taking him on with the endurance race not the sprint. Fleeces' keep em up I am gonna wop this young drips arse real good. Yeah says Vince the old guy thinks he's still got it, but he will shit himself half way through, poor old bugger! 'Hey team I am gonna wop this poor old basted real good watch this, boy was he ever wrong'?

So it's off they go first five done and Vince is ahead and laughing, come on old fella did ya drop ya balls already, Puke said nothing. Five more down now and Vince is even further ahead and still Puke says nothing, except still ten to go young fella your balls aint dropped yet. The next five done and they are neck and neck, what now hot shot, have ya shot ya bolt already laughs Puke, Vince says nothing.

'Hey hot shot yells the foreman' leave their bloody ears on this poor old bugger here has none left, what happened, did the hand piece slip. 'Hey Hot shot this one has no arse ole left' what is she supposed to do with no ring your bloody shears slip again. 'Crikey hot shot this poor old girl has tears in her eyes what did ya done to her, ya big bully ya. Never mind mate the old guy there is doin or right buddy, but ya need t hurry up yerself or ya is gonna lose Moight'.

'Hey Hot shot these fleeces are ripped to shreds' is your hand piece doing the wrong thing again. 'Hey Hot shot are you shearing or crutching Pukes gonna get ya this time hot shot serves ya bloody right, ya still shittin yella ya mug. Crikey the old fella is one in front of ya hot shot old bugger must still have it wadda ya reckon now'.

'Hey Puke these sheep o yours is happy and smiling at me did ya tickle the old girls tits, do ya have time for that Crikey, Vince looks as if his balls have gone ome home witout him this is tough stuff Moight. Hey Ray this old girl is so happy looks as if she is dancing a tango with her mate here, and they both has two ears we think she is appy cos she never got put in hot shots pen, wadda ya reckon about dat is we right orf not'?

'Hey hot shot have ya dropped ya balls he is two in front now what happened you has you big mouf shut for a change. Hey hot shot he has his last one you has two ta go whats up looks like you is gonna be wopped, mind you the poor old basted might drop dead and then you might win, but it betta be quick now. Oh yes Rays sheep all have two ears left hot shot your poor old girls have none, are you having sheep's ears for dinner tonight hot shot. Hey look the sheep is

havin a party here and voting for the shed gun even the rams aint votin for you mate, they is frightened yu might shear out their ploomin balls mate. These plurry rams are is lookin real scared dey is real scared of da prospeks wif out da balls dey might finish up at da meat works'?

'Hey hot shot Puke is nearly finished what are these two still standing in your pen are they stray or sumpin yeah they must be strays, hey but even if they are you still lost. Ya no wat Hot shot even da sheep here think yu is just a boy, dey has got wise old looks on their faces dey still love ya their young moit hot shot, but when da whips was crackin ya done ya balls tell dem da truff why doncha dey will still loves ya guarantee it'!

Vince had sweat even running down his backside, by time he did his last two Puke was leaning on his rail having a quiet cigarette. By this time Vince knew he had been conned by Puke into an endurance race not a sprint, so when he finished he said 'you bloody prick, let's do it again tomorrow with ten sheep not twenty and then I will whip your Black Butt for sure'!

Not on your sweet life laughed Puke, I done ya fair and square you're the smart one not me and you fell for it so you lose. 'Then Puke leaned over and said, yes you are the shed Gun Sonny bloody Pop Gun'.

Ocean Beach Invercargill NZ

1955: #22

Some like it hot, but the Scots come from a pretty cold country, but what they don't like is to be beaten by the blacks!

Vince had been re elected as the Union Delegate for the 1955-56 season, at the Ocean Beach meat works. Vince had lost credibility the previous year with the Scottish manager because he (Manager) had been bested Vince in . There had been a joust over a request from Vince for the company to donate eight hundred ponds to the works football club. The manager had agreed but set out terms that he thought was impossible to achieve. The Union organized by Vince achieved the goal and the manager was mortified, he had been beaten by a Maori, he a Scotsman by a damned Maori. This the new season he had been determined to get rid of Vince, the company had made a mistake in allowing this Maori to come back? The Manager was defiant when Vince accompanied by his Assistant, (an older white man) arrived at the office there was an immediate eruption. "We are only here to tell you Vince has been re elected, there is no dispute why are you so upset?" The Assistant asked in surprise.

"That little idiot isn't running this works I am, he caused enough trouble last year now you want me to accept him again, don't be ridiculous?" the manager burst out in his fine Scottish accent.

The only trouble last year was when you had to pay to support the works football team when Vince bested you over whether the company paid or not that's not trouble?" the Assistant said with a smile.

"Yes that's what I mean that damned Maori cheated and the company paid that's why, it won't happen again this year," the manager stormed in anger.

"But it's the football that gives these men an interest, they are hundreds of miles away from their families, and there is nothing to do down here in the Bluff. They are paid well we know that, but that's a two way advantage. If these Northern Maoris' didn't come way down here to this works what would you do? The population of the Bluff with families is about four hundred, and you have over a thousand men from the North. I am so sorry mister manager, but such a hassle over eight hundred pounds to keep these men here is a small cost. Much as you dislike the truth Vince has helped you, support the football for goodness sake! As you know I bring about forty men each day down from Invercargill in my old bus, you have about fifteen from the Bluff. Without at least one thousand coming from the North you would have to close down, you had best accept the Maoris' or resign, that's not Vince's fault!

At this point Vince cut in and said quietly, "Mr Manager this works will be closed as soon as we can clear the chains of lambs, and that will cost the company far more than eight hundred pounds, you can be sure of that. Now let me add that if you don't apologize for this nonsense, all of us Northern Maoris' dogs as you seem to think of us will go back North, it's your choice we won't accept your silly attitude. The Maori Battalion from which many of our family men were killed fighting for you Britishers, means we won't accept you, I emphathize the you. May we respectfully suggest you go back to your company head office in London, and stay there get your bosses to send somebody who is not racist? Finally we will give you till close of the works today. If we don't get an apology then the season for this works is finished. You might have got away with slurring your own Scot's, but not us Maoris', now it's up to you there is about five hours till closing, good day Mr; Oh and don't you ever again call me a boy, I am as much a man as you are even if only twenty YOA.

Need we say the apology was received not to Vince, but to the 90% Maori team manning those contract chains, and that manager was replaced for the following year? It seems his attitude to his Maori staff was anathema, to somebody at his head office in London.

It was less than two months after that Vince was asked to come to the office to meet with that same manager. On entering the office and courteously being invited to sit down and even offered a cup of tea and a biscuit, the change in attitude was quickly obvious.

Vince the manager started, "our freezers are all full, and the ship has arrived to load out for London. There aren't enough men down on the wharf; so they have invited us to supply workers. The Company is asking the team to supply labor for a week, if we don't help then the freezers will stop us until the wharfies' can catch up, and we will have to wait. Will you arrange a team to do that work for one week?"

"Yes I will put it to the men immediately, when do you need them to start? And what rate of pay will we be getting if one says yes the others will follow, and I will say yes?" Vince said with a smile.

"London has authorized full contract rate plus 10% for one week can you get the team to start in the morning," the manager asked it is very urgent.

The vote at the meeting was yes the team would help, but only the Maoris' actually lined up to work down at the Bluff Harbor, not one white man applied.

The team cleared that boat in record time, but not a word of thanks from their Scottish Boss. That year was the first time they processed one million sheep and lambs in that freezing and meat works. There was not one word of acknowledgement from our fine boss, but he was never seen again he went back to London, before the next season started.

Hot Dice

Some like it hot, but others just can't take the heat in the kitchen!

'It was Saturday and there was no work that day up at the slaughter shed, the game was on and had been all afternoon with the pennies outside! Spin em boy's heads or tails with three pennies. The tails had been running and Doug was way in front, but everyone was waiting for the dice no one really liked the pennies! The best the heads had been able to do was three sets, and then a blow out tails she is boys, pay tails now! Now fellas away we go again set the ring boys, were set now and away we go again, get your side bets on fellas. There will be free booze and cigarettes tonight fellas, so keep you money in ya pockets, here we go boys and its bloody tails again, she's all yours Doug! Looks like it may be your turn tonight Doug, but it's about time aint it Mate, you are the only real tailie we have, and without you there is no game we know that mate'!

Ok Puke are the guards posted, it's your turn Henry is barman tonight let the pennies spin boys; there is no place for fatso tonight fellas! He can't fit through the plurry door; he can play but no going through the emergency door! What a ya reckon Fatso we want ya to play mate, but that door is too small for you so you just wait if there is a raid, old Beale can't say you are playing by yourself now can he mate? Ok boys the rec room is all set so let's all go inside and bring ya money wit ya just bring ya money fellas!

'OK here men free beer and cigarettes Henry has it all ready for you all, we supply the cigarettes and Booze you all play the dice. If ya aint playin now just piss off there aint no room for spectators here not tonight no way?

And ok man lets go game open now men the games open play dice boys, here we go'?

The tails were running and Doug was makin a big quid, then a stranger stepped up to roll the dice! I am a headie he announced and I wanta spin em for five grand, so the game is on five grand to see the man go five grand here fill the ring first fellas, ok mate spin em. Heads she is boys

Ya leave it all in OK ten grand to see the man go heads again. that two sets boy and are ya goin again and its heads again pay heads fellas he is goin again fellas all up twenty grand to see the man go, its heads again boys and she's all up again now we need forty grand to see the man go.

Ok fellas all we is need forty grand to see the man go what are you doin Doug you are takin it all OK men the ring is set yes get ya side bets on the ring is set she all set in the ring. Yes fellas he's goin for his fourth set of heads and Doug's bettin him out you is in fo a big buck again Doug, ok let the man go crikey its heads again we have eighty grand here to see the man go whats that you say Doug, 'you want to see the dice, sure thing mate have a look as much as you look the dice is clean mate?

Hey where are you goin buddy come back here whats the problem here, come back and bring that money back here you aint the ringie here mate we are. Now put that cash back down there fella while Doug checks the dice.

'Whats that you say Doug the dice is loaded they can't be they are our dice, and we don't use loaded dice hey stay here fella and no you can't take that money'. The man says we are cheatin, but you is the stranger here not us, what is you up to here buddy, let me see those fuckin dice Doug please.

'These are not our fuckin dice Buddy what are you up to did you palm the fuckin dice if you have we will have your balls for bloody yoe yoes yes we will, bloody yoe yoes. Hey fellas this bloody stranger has palmed the dice and run us with loaded dice, he is just a bloody smart arse he is? No don't go away Buddy we are gonna fix you up for bloody cheatin we are you is gona pay we will throw you to our boys ya see they is gonna fix you real good for cheatin here. We don't like bloody cheats here you could a taken Doug here for a pile a cash tonight, we is goona fuck you properly?'

Whats the story Doug are they loaded and how, they are loaded for Heads the bloody prick. What do we do with him fellas toss him to the boys yes we will hey fellas, we have a blow in cheat here can you blokes teach him a lesson, he won't forget. You can? Good take him away but no don't cut his balls out that might cause some problems maybe he has a wife!

'Ok you have his five grand Doug and all your brass back less our commission of course, we are just glad the silly bugger tried to split, if he did not we might have been blamed. Whats that you say Doug oh you would never believe we run in a bum set of dice. Thanks mate, but you is right mate we would just ruin our game'.

Ok fellas lets play dice who is spinning now you are buddy how much one grand, no sweat see the man go fellas one grand for the centre fellas see the man go. Ok we are all set get yer side bets on fellas ok here we go, its tails boys!

The learner

1957: #24

Somes got it somes not:

Vince had been employed as a Gun (expert) Boner by a Wholesale and Contract Meat Company on trial, and had quickly proved he was capable of doing the job? His foreman and employer were both very impressed, at his speed with a knife. But this was because Vince had been a contract Boner and because of this training was very quick with a knife. Boning was now just a simple job for Vince, but he had ambitions to learn all aspects of the meat industry, including making Continental and New Zealand style Smallgoods. There was also to learn, Bacon, Ham and Salamis', Roast and Corned Beef Rolled, Retail over the Counter Service, and serving Hotels, Hospitals, Restaurants' and Chinese Cafes'. Vinces boast was he was going to be the most diversified and best man in his chosen industry! At twenty one YOA there appeared to be a good chance for him to succeed? At his age (21) he was in strong demand by others wanting to employ him, and his pay was already higher than most other tradesmen.

Vince had already learned most of the jobs and he was considered by his peers to be a Gun Boner, and an all round expert with either an eight inch, or a small boning knives. He had served his time on general farm work nurturing breeding and growing the different animals. Finally he had learned several different types of animal food growing ie Hay, Silage, Barley and Wheat etc. Vince liked his work because he found it very easy, and he could wander round most of the time when his quota had been done.

At the firm he was working for there was a specialist man (Harold) who did nothing but making rolled roasts' and corned beef. Vince used to watch Harold working out of the corner of his eye, and took good note that this fellows' product was far superior; to any of the others' who were doing the same job. When looking at the rolls hanging in the big coolers, it was easy to see the ones that had been made by this man, they were all straight and even and would cook up very well for whoever bought them. Vince was determined that he would learn to be as good. Because Vince had been contract trained working on an hourly rate was very easy, he used to bone the carcasses put up for him in about 20% of the time allowed. The rest of the time he used to wander around learning other jobs, and helping out everywhere!

Finally one day Vince walked up to Harold whose work he had been admiring, and asked if he would teach him (Vince) to do the job as well as he did. Looking at Vince in a very superior way Harold said, No it's not possible to do that because I don't believe you would have the ability to do my Job? 'It's taken me twenty years to learn this job, now my work is the best by far, so it's not possible to teach you'!

'Crikey thought Vince it has taken him twenty years to learn to do that, must be pretty dumb that fella it will take me a month to learn in my spare time? It will be my pleasure to teach that smarty a lesson on how to learn quickly'!

Vinces' work was on second grade beef all going into mince meat. When boning the second grade meats the same cuts were on the carcass but these low quality meats were all being used for mince. Saving the second grade cuts and putting some aside Vince would have several to practice on in his lunch hour making roast beef, of course because it was low grade meat his work was just for learning. He was the only one to stay in the work room at lunch time, so nobody knew what he was doing. By time the rest of the staff came back, Vince had cut his second grade roasts up and hidden them, by putting them into the mince containers. By doing this he was able to learn how the job was done, but because he could not use any prime cuts he didn't know if his product was quite as good as Harold's. Every day out of the corner of his eye he would watch Harold, and everything he did, but he made sure not to be obvious. Harold would carry on making his roasts, quite unaware he had an apprentice learning off him.

Sadly for Harold he was off one day sick and the foreman had asked Vince, if he could do roast and corned beef! Sure I can and just as well as Harold does them, my quality is guaranteed let me show you? For the first time Vince had the right material for doing a prime roast, and as he had guaranteed they turned out just as neat as Harold's!

The Foreman was impressed good he said, now I don't have to put up with that blasted Harold always telling me he is the only roast expert here. Harold was away for three days! All of that time besides doing his own work, Vince did the same amount or roasts as Harold would have done. The Foreman was delighted, but poor Harold when he finally came back to work was disappointed, he had hoped to have been badly missed! When he saw Vinces' line of roasts sitting on the cooler rail, and was told who had made them he was shocked? Never again did he speak to Vince, but never again did he try to tell all of the staff how superior he was to everyone else! Harold had learned a lesson, taking twenty years to learn such a simple job, only proved what a poor tradesman he really was.

The Blackbird

Christchurch NZ has a lot of Blackbirds and they can be really cheeky vicious brutes!

Vince was riding his bike to work at Cross Bros Butchery in Geraldine St; Albans in Christchurch New Zealand. It was 7.25am and he was to start at 7.30 so he was in a hurry, when suddenly he heard a little girl who sounded, terrified screaming. Looking toward the screams Vince could see a Blackbird Pecking at a little girl' who was cowering and screaming loudly! Riding over to the footpath dropping his bike, he then walked up and kicked the bird from behind, allowing the girl to run off into the house whimpering. The bird hopped away defiantly not even trying to fly and looked at Vince, but then decided he was too big to attack so flew off. Vince did not try to follow the girl, he had done what he intended to do now he went to work and arrived a little late.

The suburbs of Christchurch abound with Blackbirds, but this one was extremely aggressive, it was obvious the girl would have been quite injured had Vince not happened along! Vince forgot the incident and continued on to work, which was only about one hundred yards away. He did not even report the matter to the job foreman because he considered the matter insignificant, he was wrong! The only comment that was made was, that he had been a few minutes late getting to work that morning. Vince was renowned for arriving a minute before starting time, on that day he was five minutes late.

The next day at work there was a call over the loudspeaker for Vince to come up to the office immediately there was a visitor to see him. Surprised Vince did as requested and was even more surprised to see two big police men waiting for him. Are you they asked Vincent Stephens of 9 Slater Street St. Albans? And do you ride a bicycle to work in the morning at about 7.30am. All this was asked with Vinces' Boss sitting listening?

The answer to the questions was all yes, so Vince was happy to agree that what they were asking was correct! He then asked why they wanted to know and if there was anything else? He had to get back to work because there were orders to be filled, and the delivery van was waiting for him to complete his part of the work? Having thus explained himself he politely waited for the police reaction!

We are the police said, investigating the claim that you molested a little girl on your way to work yesterday at about 7.25-30am; and we are here to pick you up for investigation. Will you pick up whatever you need and come with us to the St Albans Station?

Pick me up for investigation, it was me that saved that little girl how silly can you be, you should be bringing me a present from her parents? This annoys me the child was being badly attacked by an angry Blackbird which was kicked by me, that saved her! Now you want to pick me up what is this really, because I am a Maori? Why the hell would I want to molest a little girl, couldn't they see the bird's marks on her arms, and I don't have a beak with which to inflict that type of injury. Do you have an arrest warrant or not, to me it seems more like victimization because I am a northerner'.

That will be enough of your cheek Stephens the police Sergeant said, we still need to take you away to consider this report and to have you make out a statement. Turning to Vinces' boss and with a big smile on their faces they said. Sorry Mr. Cross but this man is suspected of assault on a minor, and he is to be interrogated. As you will realize he is a Northern Maori, and we do have a lot of trouble with them types. He may or he may not be back at work tomorrow, it depends on what evidence he can provide to confirm he is innocent of the allegations by this little girls parents'.

Much to Vinces' surprise his boss said this charge if charge it is, is silly, Vince is a highly respected employee here and it will be my pleasure to vouch for his integrity. Let me add he has a very beautiful Wife, at home and believe me has no need to molest girls' either big or small. Now officers' may I suggest you go back to the child's parents' and ask them to check their child's story. Whatever the child says there is no way this man would be interested in molesting her.

The next morning the call came again for Vince to come up to the office! This time the police were accompanied by another well dressed man, who was obviously the child's father.

Bill Cross was sitting in his office padded chair with a big smile on his face. Looking at the stranger and pointing at Vince he said, this is the man who saved your daughter you need to thank him! It is a difficult thing to be accused of such a thing as molesting a little girl, and could have ruined this young man's' reputation, except we know him well.

Yes we know, and that's correct said the man, our Daughter was hysterical and we misunderstood what she was saying. We had a doctor come and sedate her and we know now we wrongly accused you of molestation, my Wife and myself are deeply sorry. He held out his hand to Vince, it was taken and the two shook hands the matter was ended.

The police men then turned to Vince and said you are indeed lucky to have such a boss, a big mistake was almost made. Both of them then shook hands with Vince and left.

Vince only ever had one question, when he wandered did Bill Cross ever see my Wife?

The night man

Not a job many could do, but for Vince he money smelt fine and the job was very well paid, guess it had to be or none would do the stinkin job!

The job had been offered to Vince as a bet and a joke, by the foreman at his day job work place. Knowing Vince wanted a spare time job he had challenged him to work on the Night Soil Truck, and the bet was he would not last the first night. The Boss of the truck was a Bill Luke, and he had been a Night Soil Contractor in Christchurch for over thirty years. This was the last truck working! Nearly all of Christchurch was now on the sewer, and it was expected that within five years, all of the rest would be as well? The routine was to be, that Bill would pick Vince up at his home put his bike in the back of the car, and when the round was finished he was to ride home. Bill would go down to the Bromley sewer farm, empty and steam hose the truck a one man job! Special clothes were provided big heavy gloves for protection, and finally heavy pads for the shoulders, on which the 'over sized sewer can' is carried.

The first house Vince had to pick up was almost a disaster, struth he thought looks like I am going to lose that bet. Bill stood outside the house and explained where to go and how to carry the can? Vince was very strong anyhow so he had no problem lifting and carrying the can, which at times was well over sixty five kilos! Vince went in as told, but the sight of the sewage and the awful smell was enough to turn his stomach! Crikey he was thinking as he walked out to the truck and emptied the contents, this is ploomin tough stuff. The work was not hard but the smell of it, was what was hard to overcome!

How are yer goin with it mate asked Bill with a laugh! Crikey this is shit galore or right, stinks worse than me feet after a hard game of footie! I blocked me nose and shoved the stinkin can on me shoulder and here I am master shit man I be. They both laughed and Bill explained the next load. (House)

After a few houses had been done Vince had got the routine and become used to the stink, there was no more trouble, but he still didn't fancy it as a job? At the end of the night when Bill paid him Vinces' aversion to the job vanished, struth for that pay no wonder you have been doing this for so long, so would I? How many nights do you want me to work? Four answered Bill we only go out those nights now, and it's getting less all of the time, but yes financially it's been good to me? The only trouble is my wife shares my cheque book, they both laughed.

From then on the four nights the routine was the same, but sometimes there were problems, like when the bottom fell out of a house can. Usually when the can had become too old and was badly eroding, then a big mess was left for the occupants to clean up. The cans were expensive and usually it was because the occupants could not afford to buy a new one, was why they had let the old one stay for too long?

They were very quick to renew though once the bottom fell out and they had to clean up the mess! About 50% of those old toilets were in the houses! Vince could never understand how they could live with that awful smell right inside their homes. On that job it was easy to see the habits of some of the people as being dreadful and dirty.

One night they were doing a few houses at the one stop, when a bloke came out and said, hurry up and bugger off you blokes stink like hell? Vince asked, do you smell that real bad one above over the rest. No he answered! Well it's your stink it's even worse than all the rest do you live on garlic, because you really stink buddy! The bloke slunk of suitably chastised, followed by a laugh from Bill and Vince.

One night some persons left a rope over the path way, put up after Vince went in. But as he passed he could hear giggling so knew something was going to happen on the way out, and it did. Some teenagers living in the house had stretched a rope over the path, expecting Vince to spill the sewage over himself. Vince pretended to slip and threw the full can of sewage down over the path, in front of him. First there was the start of big laughs from inside, turning to cries of dismay as they realized what had happened. None had fallen on the night man but all had fallen over their path and lawn, now it was Vince laughing.

One night Vince did trip and spilt some urine over himself that was a dreadful night's work. When he got home, his wife who always waited up to run the bath for him, insisted he undress while she ran the hose over him and bathed him with disinfectant.

Xmas time was a bonanza on the Night Cart every house left out a present, they dare not in fear the night man may tip their sewage for that night over the garden? Of course that would not have happened, but it was a myth both were happy to perpetuate. The presents were mostly liquor of high quality Whisky, Gin and Vodka etc; Vince never drank alcohol not even beer so his presents were all sold to workmates.

Gradually the old night truck was phased out first down to three nights then two, and finally after three years it was all over. The old poop cart was no more it was all over finally Christchurch was all on the sewer!

Our First Home

1957: #27

Sometimes it's foolish to judge to quickly, had he chose Vince could have paid cash for the bloody house!

What does a man do when he is told by his Wife their first child is on the way? In my case it was well guess we better buy a house, this little flat won't be big enough. We had moved into a small flat at 9 Slater St Albans with Mrs. Alexander and her Son Gerald, but now reluctantly it was time to move on? At the time neither my Wife nor I knew how to go about buying a house, so we figured the thing to do was ask a Real Estate Agent. The next day from work we picked out of the phone book an agent, and made an appointment for him to come to our little flat, later in the week.

In the meantime we both spent our time looking around Christchurch and asking what the prices were like. It was obvious there would be no trouble buying a house, but we did not really know how to go about getting what we wanted. We waited for the Agent with some excitement knowing this was to be our first home, and our first child was soon to arrive it was great. What can be more exciting than getting that first home, nothing except getting the first child, that tops it all off.

That night the door bell rang and my Wife answered to the expected Agent, and bought him into our lounge room. My Wife a White girl was greeted quite civilly when she answered the door, but when he saw me his attitude changed. "What he asked in a surly voice do you want, you know this is difficult getting me to come out at night? Do you realize I am a married man with children, when we work at night, it's only if the clients are important you sounded important, but this is nothing but a waste of my time.

It was obvious he had a problem with me, but it was nothing new so his attitude was ignored at that point. "Why I said we want to buy a house what else do you think we rang you for, we told you when we rang what we wanted? If you think it's a waste of time well then buzz of, we can go somewhere else no problem".

"And how do you intend to pay for this house, you need money you know?" he said very sourly. "Any house is very expensive and everybody has to have the cash to pay for what they want to buy, you have to show me your money first."

"Why we intend to borrow the money how else do you think we would pay for it, borrow of course and as quickly as possible?" I said with a big confident smile. In fact we had a considerable amount of money on fixed deposit more than enough to pay cash, but we didn't want to tell the agent.

"Not from me you don't, we don't lend money to Maoris' we know we won't get it back, and I suppose you are from the North Island as well which is even worse he said with a sneer and look of contempt. You Northern Maoris' come down here and are just a lot of trouble, it would be better if you all stayed in Auckland that's where Maori are welcome not down here".

Knowing my always volatile temper my Wife hastened to usher my new friend out and he left with the sneer still on his face. My Wife politely said to him as he left that have should be more careful when dealing with customers, because now he had lost a sale.

His reply was there was no sale here because we would never be able to borrow any money; Maoris' were not accepted as borrowers. My Wife was tempted to tell him the truth, but decided that would upset me even further it was not worth the problem.

The next day Vince and his Wife went down to the Building Society where there was deposited enough money to pay cash, and told them what had happened. Don't worry they said, you made a mistake any Real Estate Agent would embrace you had you told them your position. There are not many couples of either race who have what you have on deposit with us, but the Agent did not know that. Had you told him he would have been all over you to sell you a house?

"No our affairs are private we protested why should we tell them what we have or have not got? He was just an ignorant sod anyhow we prefer privacy let them think we have nothing who cares," said Vince.

"Well just tell any Agent to ring us, and we will tell them they can sell you any house you want, and we will tell them we will pay for it. That means they don't need to know any of your business hows that? But you can buy any where here in Christchurch even in Fendalton if you wish?" said our advisor".

Thinking then to be a smart Alec we rang the Agent of the previous night and told him what the building Society had said.

What a change in attitude there was, Mr. Stephens he said, "We have several beautiful homes on our books, let me come around again tonight and show you. It will be my pleasure to show you all around the city and suburbs, when can we pick you up?"

Yeah well it seems to me you don't like Maoris' it's just me telling you that a sale has been missed because you were a smart Alec good bye now. Oh and the money is mine not my Wife's so don't you think that I am bludging on her. Maoris' are not as bad as you think bye now.

Another home

1958: #28

Anything is possible if the price is right!

It was a surprise arriving home to be told my Son, now six months old was to be enrolled in a private church college. How are we supposed to pay for that, that's the second most expensive college here, my wages wont stretch that far! That's ok I will work and help, but our Sons must have the best. What do you mean Sons we only have one, are you hoping for more Sons, thanks but for me we need to have a couple of girls next.

Ok have it your way, but Brent is booked in to this school, and they start in the primers right through to year twelve. It's good because he will be the first Maori going to this school from Tiny Tots to University Entrance. The only thing is we will have to buy another house, so he can walk to school it's too far away from here to walk.

Struth the poor little fella is only six months old. And we have to buy a new house now so he can walk to school, that's not a bad trick. You are pretty smart alright you book him into an expensive school and then side track my thoughts, by talking about a new house, you should be the company's salesgirl. You could really get the sales way up you have more diversion tricks than anyone else I have ever known that's for sure.

Do you want to come and see the Tiny Tot teacher my Wife asked, her name is Mrs. Joyce and she has been there for years, she is very nice and runs the junior school. When they showed me through the school they introduced me to Mrs. Joyce she is a wonderful teacher.

So you gleaned all of this out of a school meeting, at which you booked our Son in as a Tiny Tot and you then blithely tell me all about a new house etc. This is unbelievable at least since it's me that has to pay the bills; it might be nice to know what debts there will be in future. Look in future can you at least tell me before you set me up with more debt. We have just bought a house what do we intend to do with that one may I ask?

Oh we will split that up into flats and get a good income; I have a quote for the job it should be here in a few days.

No that's out of the question I will have to build that myself, it will cost too much to have a contractor do the job. When and if we find another house will be when we will price the conversion costs into two flats, one three and one two bedrooms.

But let me warn you do not start looking for another house yet, because we need to wait until we have more money in the bank. There is no way we are going into big debts, I want our money to stay in the bank you know that. Oh sorry what was meant is, if you listened to me you would know!

Two weeks later his Wife rang and said, there is a house over by the college for sale, they only want two thousand four hundred pounds that is a wonderful price. It's is so very cheap dear and you know the money is in the bank, so why should we be worried there won't be any debt?

Good grief why will you not listen we are not wealthy people, I am just twenty two years of age, and you want to send our son to a College we cannot afford. Before the child can even walk you want to buy another house, for goodness sake give me a break; it's not my way to have next to nothing in the bank.

Anyhow we went to see this new house at 69 Searells Rd Papanui, the Real Estate Agent as usual was full of superlatives, he could sense a sale. Vince's Wife was waffling on about how good and cheap the darn house was. Look they both said only two thousand four hundred pounds, and then as listening to them a bright idea came to Vince.

OK so the price is as you say but it's not worth the money not by a long way, let me make an offer. We are offering one thousand six hundred pounds walk in walk out that's our first and only offer, and the owner has two weeks to accept or reject. Boy that's smart I thought to myself now everybody is happy, I don't want this house but there is an offer in. My Wife won't be able to whine and she might not be so quick to find another, because that type of offer is all they will get of me.

The Agent brightly said there is no way they will sell for that silly price, at two thousand you might get a buy but not at that price! It would be easy to sell this house for two thousand pounds, we have to be fair to the Vendor and your offer is not fair.

Well that's the best that we can offer it's a cash offer and we will settle in seven days, we have the money in the bank. Sure the price is cheap but the money to settle is quick can't have it both ways it is a fair offer.

A week later Vince's Wife rang again, well we got the house she said with a delighted sound in her voice, can you send them a cheque please, for the deposit straight away.

Oh hell that smart move has collapsed that was Vince's first thought. His second thought was crikey that's a cheap buy so he said into the phone, sure Dear where do I take the cheque to? When will they have the contract ready?

Buying a Factory

1959: #29

Who wants to buy that old heap of Junk why me of course.

Vince answers the phone: Sure Bill so you want to have a meeting with me, what for Buddy? Do you have a nice present for me or something? You what you want to sell me your old factory don't be silly! Why would we want that old hunk of junk? You have built a new place and now you want me to buy your left over's? What you will leave in the old equipment, that's only fit to be sold for scrap iron anyhow! Pardon me? You will make me an offer we can't resist? Struth! So you are giving me that hunk of rubbish for nothing? There must be something wrong! Yes I know the land is worth something not much but something. Tell me the truth Bill, what you really mean is you want me to leave my job and that means John won't be able to compete for the contracts. That's pretty cute Bill you sell your old junk and cut out your competition, and I finish up with some rubbish we can sell for scrap metal!

No! We are not really interested Bill. Sorry mate, but it's not your day for setting traps for foolish ex staff members. You should have paid me the proper wage in the first place and then I would still be on your meat production foreman. Whats that? You will let me have the lot for sixteen thousand pounds? You must be black Santa Claus mate, anyhow we don't have any money so it's not even the price. Me not be a monkey mate me see no money me no buy, tank you berry much for your kind offer Santa but me tinkit a bad deal ok.

Hello? Oh it's you again Bill! Gee! We will have to stop meeting like this; my Wife will get jealous Mate, what can we do for ya Moit? You what?

You will take only twelve thousand pounds, even though the land is worth more than that? Tell ya what; just bulldoze the old dump down then, and sell the land to some idiot for that money, you might find a nut with that much money to give away. What's that you say? There will never be another bargain like this one offered to me? Crikey! That's just as well! The stress of such an offer would be too much! No mate! There is no way we worked together for too long, no I wouldn't trust you to walk my old dog around the block, you might pinch the poor old bugger and turn him into mince meat.

Hello again Bill! You want to make me another offer? But that's not what I said. What was said is no, we don't want that old dump! What's that you say now? It's down to ten thousand pounds. Crikey! If we had any money we might think about it Bill, such a shame we are just paupers. Ya, No, yes if we had the money at that price we would buy that old junk.

Hi Bill! This must mean the price is down to eight thousand! Crikey! You is getting close now! Whats that? No, it's still ten grand, but we already said no at that price! Didn't ya hear me Moit? It's a great big no! 'Cos we aint got no money, I told ya that Moit.

You will what? Oh! You will carry the mortgage, gee that's generous mate! Ten thousand interest free for how long did you say? Oh you did not say no interest, well the deals still no! Then why, do you want interest that's only a taxable income? The money we will pay you as capital is tax free that's why we are happy to pay more than the place is worth, let's face it six thousand is the real value! We are paying four thousand too much but its tax free, that's a good deal for you. We have never been so generous before, that is 'cos you are a special friend and it's nice doing business with you Bill. OK so you will let us have the mortgage interest free; yes it's better that way we have built the price up between us, and now its real value! What's that you say Bill? You say we are thieves? That's not very nice to say about an old employee Bill! Be nice because we like you Bill.

Hi Bill, it's me Vince, you know me your real Santa Claus just checking you did say that mortgage was for ten years interest only? Oh! You didn't say that Bill? Oh gosh! And I thought we had a deal! Never mind! That's just the way it works sometimes, sorry! It's like me old girl friend, she didn't know the difference between yes and no either. Oh well, whats that you say Bill? You will agree to ten years, like me old girl friend ya know, its yes again? Crikey mate! What? Don't call you Mate? Why not? We have been Mates for ten years so what's your problem now? Whats that? You will send the contracts to my lawyers? Oh no, you won't! I aint paying one of those sharks! You have to pay all of that rubbish! OK Bill we have a deal at last! Why did you have to come up with all of the bulldust? It would have been much easier for me without all of the fuss ya know.

What's that funny noise Bill? Oh! It's you crying because you was a virgin, and you aint never been screwed before? No! That's not true I am heterosexual ask my wife, why doncha. Anyhow you is an ugly brute Bill, there aint no way any of the boys would be interested in you; no way.

What's that you say? You want to go and have a good cry? Let's go down and have a beer Mate, oh! It's your shout! I shouted last time, and crikey Mate yo is crying?

Anzac Day two up

1956 : #30

Here we go the moneys' on the table and we is all hot ta trot!

Dollar values as in 2008.

The three partners were meeting before the night's game Vince, Henry and Ray. The big games on tonight; and we have cut an escape route out of the games room the entry doors a little narrow, but if the police raid us there will be time for the players to go through one by one. There will be about one hundred players coming tonight including a couple of high roller TAILLIE bettors so it should be a good night. The big game has started there is over one hundred players and there is plenty of money on the tables. The HEAD bettors are way ahead but the TAILLIES are not running out of cash. Ok now it's my turn to take over the table, so here we go.

Ok fellas we have a $5,000 in the ring give me a cover all or part of this $5,000 ok the ring is covered now get your side bets on. All set ok spinner roll the dice now, yes boys its heads players pay heads.

The spinner is staying in with his full stake so its $10,000 to go. Yes fellas' $10,000 in the ring please, no side bets until the ring is set. Ok all set in the ring get your side bets on. Ok all set on the side roll em spinner. Heads again fellas, the ring pays heads.

Watch it you tails bettors spinner is backing himself to throw his third set of heads and he's staying with his full stake so its $20,000 needed in the ring. Here we go set the ring first bettors set the ring first. OK bettors the ring is set at $20,000 so get your side bets on. Ok players all bets set so, come in spinner here we go Bettors and it's heads again, three set of heads in a row Bettors. Heads are hot players, heads are hot the ring pays heads again.

Come on players spinner is going again with the lot so we need $40,000 in the ring. Watch it now players the ring must be set before there is any side bets taken, come on TAILLIES we need $40,000 for the ring set the ring first players. This is the fourth set of heads see the man go. Ok all set in the ring get you side bets on players here we go now, come in spinner see the dice roll players. Goodness gracious me we have heads again pay the man that's his fourth set of heads' hard luck TAILLIES, but it's heads again pay the man please.

Oh my the man wants to run again how are you going Doug we need $80,000 to see the man go are you chasing your dough Doug. Come on you TAILLIES see the man go players we need $80,000 come on you TAILLIES see the man go players. Ok the ring is all set to go, now any side bets get your side bets on are we all set? Ok roll them spinner let those dice go spinner.

Crikey players it's heads again pay the heads players that's the game fellas' this guy is hot fellas' that's his fifth set of heads man this guy is real hot five sets of heads fellas' how are you TAILLIES going do you all want to go again this guy is hot.

Ok players our man wants to go again he has a big dream to flatten you TAILLIES so now it's $160,000 needed in the ring can we fill the ring players no side bets we need the money all in the ring. NO side bets players we need it all in the ring we need $160,000 to see the man go. How are you going Doug are you still in or is this man too hot he is going for his sixth set. Ok you TAILLIES got no more money the rings not set yet still calling for money ok thanks Doug we have the money to go again come in Spinner he's spinning for $320,000 players if he gets a head he has all of the money. Now come in Spinner for your last shot, bloody hell it's another head the man has done it he has the lot.

The spinner wants to go again anybody here want to take all or part of the ring and we have $320,000 in the ring no takers are you all sure this bloke wants to be sure you have all had a fair go Ok players is it all over. Doug whats that you say, your house is worth $400,000 no debt and you want to put it up against the ring. Yes the spinner accepts that bet Doug. So this is the last Spin players for this man and he is going for number six, any side bets before we see the man go. Here we go players and it's a tails hard luck spinner and you're off the hook Doug good on you mate here is the cash less our commission of course.

Bloody hell it's a police raid now take it easy boys there plenty of time just one at a time now. Hey whats the holdup out there. You say there's a fat guy and he is stuck in the door and nobody can get past him. Struth kick his fat butt then, we have to get these players out. What he is stuck can't get out and can't get back hell hurry or we are all gonna get done.

Too late the cops are here and they have us all except Doug he went before the fat guy.

Don't worry fellas' we will pay all of the fines, but no we can't fix the coppers sorry.

Old Sergeant Beale from the Bluff thinks it's party time he got over 120 players, cos we let a fat guy get in our escape route first. "Hey there Sergeant it's Anzac Day give it a break?"

Accounting in Christchurch

1956: #31

One plus one equals three:

It was getting boring in Christchurch because there was not enough work to do; Vince had work from 8.00am until 5.00pm less one hour for lunch eight hours per day! He had a job cutting electrical wire channels for the remodeling of St Elmo's Court in Amagh St Christchurch, but that's all he had to do. He was one day reading the NZ Herald and noticed an advertisement for a Home Accounting Course Sponsored by the Auckland University. That looks ok he thought so applied immediately, and in a short time had all of the material to start learning accounting?

It was all really easy, he sent in the tests and got very good marks, but he found all he wanted to learn was tax? The tests were just so easy he wasn't bothered with completing them! He did do a few of the tests but then got bored and only did the tax tests. The University sent a letter telling him he was doing well, and that he should sit the exams. Vince sent back a letter saying he was not interested any longer, and he was pulling out effective immediately? That meant he has never been qualified, he is just a carpet bagger in the true sense of that phrase!

From the tax papers he had learned what he wanted he then set out to minimize his tax, he set up a small business as a commercial cleaner. The first thing was to get some cleaning contracts, he won three. The Royal Society in Herford St, The Dental Surgery in Colombo St and Gainsworth Fashions in Ferry Rd. These were all destined to be loss contracts for several years! All of the other incomes could be manipulated legally, so that his total income was consolidated and the cleaning losses deducted? The other work he got was the morning load out at the Abattoirs every morning starting at 4.00am until 7.00am, the Night Cart finishing at 2.00am four days a week, Cleaning all weekend for eighteen hours, Killing lambs at the Abattoirs six hours per day, and casual work at Verkerks meat four hours per day, all up one hundred and seven hours per week and he did that from 1956-1959 until after his first son was born.

The lessons he had learned on his accounting course that related to tax enabled him to pay no tax at all and do that all legally! This work plus the money he had earned working in the meat works as a contractor was how he had the money when needed to set up Vinads'! This confounded the critics who thought Vinads' had no money, they were in fact money and tax effective from the start. Having no money was what Vince always said when he was crying poor man all of the time.

Some great bargains had been bought because of Vinces' constant refrain, but we aint got no money while his accounts were getting very fat for years! When he bought some of the properties they owned, his claims of no money made people who were anxious to sell to believe him, and he got great bargains which only added to their wealth?

When he immigrated to Australia, it was the tax knowledge, he had used to great effect when building the management consultancy in Sydney, that he ran for thirty five years very successfully! He did not set out to do what he did, it was a surprise when clients kept coming and asking for his services. It was only after the practice had been created that Vince realized what he had, and that was a professional Public Officer practice? At the start the tax dept was a little wary of Vince, because he had such an intimate knowledge of each clients business and always won any claims he made on their behalf argument, but eventually he won their respect!

Very often over the years he was asked if he was qualified and he answered no and don't want to be, when asked why he replied? First if qualified one is a servant of the State and there cannot be two masters, it's either the client or the State, I chose the Clients.

If one becomes a CPA or other such Accounting organization you have another boss, the Accountants Profession setting up rules etc. If we had chosen to be affiliated with the say CPA and answerable to the Tax Office that puts the clients third, that's not for me.

How he used to be asked do you then do your work with the tax office if you are not registered easy? Easy was the reply! We have fifteen company clients, and we are the registered Public Officer for each one. That position means we are the administrator responsible for each and every client, so the tax dept sees us as legal managers within the law, which we are? This means we have the responsibility to make sure the accounts are up to date and always legal; the tax dept has already proved up our technical correctness? For several years the Public Officer could also act in Court for their clients, but now that has been challenged by the Law Society, and has been cancelled? Over the thirty years of working in Australia we had built up a practice for being Professional Public Officers, and it's been very successful.

There have been many times when fully Qualified Accountants have rung Vince for advice even though, they know we aren't qualified, hows that? We have also had disputes with many lawyers, but never lost a case in court. The same applies to the Tax Dept, we have never lost a commercial case, we did lose a retail case, but that was because we were into something we did not know! We retired from the business when they bought in GST Vince figured he was too old to learn all over again and it was time to give it all away!

That's what came from that Accounting course so many years ago that was just used to get specific knowledge and then tossed away.

Oysters Galore

1958; #32

How many Bluff Oysters could Vince eat each day, one dozen?

The season had started and Shadbolt the Oyster king of Christchurch, had received his first loads from the Bluff Oyster boats. The season lasted for six months every year, and it was the time most Oyster eaters loved the most! Vince loved Oysters' but the darn things were too expensive, so he decided to become a casual oyster opener down at Shaddies! All he really wanted was to get a free feed, but might as well earn a bit of cash once he had learned to open quick enough. Vince knew Shadbolt and knew he would get a start as a learner, but he also knew that opening oysters was not really the type of job he wanted to do? He had already mastered contract meat work (one hundred per day) a Gun. He was a fair but not a Gun Shearer, only a two hundred a day man; a gun could do from three to four hundred a day! Vince figured that within another two seasons he could lift his tally to three hundred a day, but never four hundred.

The job of contract opening Oysters seemed just too easy to master; one has to make a special knife out of any old kitchen one? The knife is filed off down to about twenty five inches then shaped into a slightly sharp, rounded end, with which to lip the Oyster. The action is to place the oyster in the palm of the hand left or right, and just run the knife around the end opposite the hinge of the shell. The Oyster is still alive and will slightly loosen its hinge when it feels the knife, and that's enough to quickly slice open the shell? A quick scoop and the Oysters are removed and sitting on the end of the knife, another quick flip and it's in the can. Payment is by the bag full, so much is paid for each bag delivered to the openers stand. There were over forty full time openers, and another thirty casuals like Vince, all told seventy openers working in that contract Oyster shed? Vince being well known in the area, knew almost every man who was there working for Shaddie.

It took Vince about one hour to get used to the action and he could open one sack per hour, two bags an hour is considered to be a gun speed. It took him another hour to learn the total action, one in the can for Shaddie and the next one into his mouth for himself? This is he thought going to be a great job, as he finished his first two bags! He had eaten a bag of Oysters and put one in for Shaddie. But Shaddie would have to pay him for two bags, WOW this is great stuff, long may Shaddie keep these Oysters coming.

Anyhow he had enough for today so from then he put them all in for Shaddie, by the end of the day he had opened six bags! Five had gone into Shaddie and one into Vinces' stomach good stuff, tomorrow I will aim for eight bags in this time, seven for Shaddie and one for me. The next day as he had figured he did the quota he had set himself and eaten another bag, his stomach was again delighted.

Crikey this is real easy thought Vince as he finished for the day, tomorrow we will aim for nine bags, eight for Shaddie and one for me? It will take me only about another week to reach two bags an hour, but must keep that one bag for me? Because of the other work he was doing Shearing and Slaughtering Sheep and Lambs, Vinces' hand were already hardened so the effect of the Oyster knife on his palms was minimal? First Vince would go out to the Abattoirs and do his tally on Lambs, then when they finished daily at 2.00pm he would ride his bike down to Shaddies. He would reach Shaddies by about 2.30pm and open until 8.30pm six hours.

Finally he had reached the target of two bags per hour and one for himself, he could now eat comfortably a bag of Oysters a day, about forty dozen! But what the hell they were free and Shaddie had to pay him for the bag he ate as well as the rest, he was now a Gun Oyster Opener? Sadly that was not how Shaddie saw the situation, he seemed to object to Vinces' ability to eat a bag of Oysters a day?

When after two weeks it was obvious that Vince could eat a sack full of Oysters' indefinitely he came to Vince and fired him, much to Vinces' annoyance? Your appetite is too much for me, we thought you would get sick of Oysters, everyone has a feed maybe a couple of dozen daily to start with, but then get sick of them you are insatiable and we cannot afford you, so take a hike young man friend or not. How the hell can anyone eat a bag of Oysters once let alone every day, you are just a glutton, eating forty dozen a day is unbelievable? How the hell do you know how many I eat a day asked Vince? By the number that comes of this stand how else ya damned guts!

But I am a gun opener now, it's silly you don't sack the guns, bloody hell I can do two bags an hour easy now, whats yer problem? Yeah you are gun but a bigger gun eating the darn things we have never had someone who could eat so many Oysters, day in and day out so bugger off Stephens? Sadly Vince packed his swag, and left, the only time in his life he had been sacked it was not nice! But oh well it was good while it lasted! It took months to get over his new found appetite for Bluff Oysters, by the sack full, or forty dozen a day?

Rotorua Penny Divers

1955: #33

Aint you blokes got any pride, our Maoris' Ancestors won the Treaty of Waitangi through war, now we, their descendants dive for penny's' thrown by Pakehas' shame on us all!

The new lamb season was nearly ready to start Vince was going by car to the Bluff; stopping first at Hastings to do two months work at the Whakatu works! After that they were going to try and get a start at the Gear meat works in Wellington, and then it was to be on to Ocean Beach meat works until July. The Bluff was always the most favorite stop, and was usually for six to eight months depending on the beef availability in Southland. On the way down it was to be a holiday in Rotorua, even though that was not Vinces' most favorite spot in New Zealand. Vince was to be traveling in a fellow workers car, Tommy was his name and the two had hopes of a good journey together.

This was not to be Tommy and Vince were not compatible. Vince was aggressive and wanted to do everything his own way, Tommy was quiet and a person no one ever noticed? Vince was just the opposite he could not help but be noticed, and was always in the fore front of everything, by the time they got to Whakatu in Hastings, they were already sick of each other? Struth Vince was thinking we have another two months together yet, what the hell are we going to do, this bloke gives me a pain in the butt?

Anyhow the trip to Rotorua was on and they left Auckland at 4.00am arriving in Rotorua at about 9.00am after a slow trip! Neither man was in a hurry so the stops for food etc; was more than normal, as usual they could smell Rotorua about an hour before they arrived? They were booked into a motel and were too early; this meant they had to wait before they could check in for the week. The next day they toured the scenic attractions of which there are quite a few, and then later in the day joined a group of Australian tourists, around the hot springs ending with the European style derelict houses that were set up at the exit! In those days guide Rangi was still alive and she was ushering us around, all went well until the group arrived at the exit or the final stages?

When we got to the old houses Guide Rangi said, and these are the type of houses our people lived in etc! This was to Vince most demeaning, he had never seen such low cast housing for their tribe and was quick to dispute with Guide Rangi, her assertions that this style house was for Maoris'. After his foolish tirade, Vince was quickly regretful and said so, he simply said he had been surprised by the houses, and was sorry for his outburst. Guide Rangi accepted his apology gracefully and the tour was over, but Vince's outburst was not. The next episode was at the bridge with the penny divers, Vince really let go here, asking how the hell Maoris' were ever going to get respect if all they did was dive for the white man's pennies, this time he would not apologize just took off in a temper.

The next day all Vince wanted to do was get out of that stinking town, but they stayed the week because their Motel was paid for, and Whakatu had not yet started. When the week was up they both decided to go to Gisborne, and have a look at the Bay of Plenty, before they started the new season.

On arrival in Hastings they had both gone to a party at Bridge Pa, and Vince even though he drank no booze had a great time! Tommy just sat there guzzling beer all night, sitting drinking and saying nothing! Vince was thinking what a boring fellow he is why did we ever think of traveling together! Tommy was probably thinking the same, what a noisy barsted this Stephens bloke is and who could blame him? There were girls everywhere and Vince talked to them all, by the time they left that party Vince wanted to stay, but it was Tommy's car so he had no choice, but to leave when Tommy did but he was brassed off!

The works at Whakatu started a week later which was just as well, Vince and Tommy were both getting so bored and sick of each other; they needed to be working so they could sweat off the animosity. The Whakatu works was an easy one to work at and unlike the Southern works were manned by locals, not itinerants such as Vince and Tommy! Vince had no responsibilities at Whakatu works, unlike Ocean Beach which had become his base, and where he had so much influence? At Whakatu he was just another Maori as were 90% of the rest of the staff, the big difference here was just that the leaders were Whites, and they controlled the works and the accommodation camp.

There was parties every week at Bridge Pa, the usual thing was to all put in money for a full keg of beer and lots of tucker, as the kegs ran out a collection would be taken to fill er up again mate? The Party usually started on Friday Night if there was no work on Saturday! If there was work on Saturday it all started on Saturday night, but never mind when they started it would finish on Monday morning in time to go to work.

Every Monday one could guarantee a lot of bleary eyed Maoris working the contract chain at the Whakatu works! There were always loads of girls at the parties, we never knew where the hell they all came from but they did, and they stayed all week end too.

Vince was sorry to leave Whakatu it was a great shed and the people were great, but the real work was calling and they had to go! The one consolation was he would soon be rid of Tommy, and of course Tommy would be rid of Vince.

Working for Verkerks

1961: #34

It was strange at first the other staff only spoke Dutch, so Vince had to talk to himself all day!

Vince had gone into Christchurch to pay the electricity bill for his home, and was surprised to see a new Butcher shop had opened up, over the road from the electricity office he was going to! The shop had for many years been operated by the Newmarket Meat Company, but their shop had been shifted around the corner to Colombo St the main road. The new owners were Vekerks Meat and Smallgoods, including Bacon and Ham. Vince was intrigued so went over to have a look in the new shops window! There were several products he did not recognize hanging on the rails, so he went in and asked what they were. He was told Frankfurters, Roqwurst etc and that they were all Dutch style sausages! He bought some frankfurters to taste and they were delicious!

It was only a few days later that Verkerks advertised for a Boner spare time, and Vince applied for and got the job. As usual he was given a trial and then accepted. He agreed to work up to twenty hours per week. It was soon obvious that Verkerks was a very diverse processor of all the meat systems that Vince wanted to learn. Watching and listening might give him the sound knowledge of the meat industry, as he had always wanted! This job was more boring than usual because the only language spoken was Dutch, and for Vince he felt isolated? There were two events that changed things for him, and made him a favorite of the owner Aalt Verkerk!

After being at the job for about five months, he suddenly wanted to go to the toilet, but had no idea where it was! He happened to be standing next to Aalt Verkerk and asked where is the toilet please Boss? What you have been here this long and don't know where the toilet is how come? That is the most popular place in this building replied Verkerk!

It has not been needed up until now, but today I need to go do you have one, and can you point out the way please? asked Vince. Oh certainly there's one sorry said the Boss and pointed it out with a smile, where it was. Watch out for all of the cigarette butts he said, that place creates more smoke than our smoke houses!

At Xmas the firm handed out four Kilo boxes chocolates to all of the staff! Thinking they might have made a mistake giving him one because he was only a casual, he went to ask Verkerk if he had made a mistake. He was assured there was no mistake, so thanked him for the present. Verkerks response was you are a strange fellow Vince! First you work here and do not understand a word of what is being said! Then you don't use the toilet for about five months, we gave forty boxes of those chocolates away for Xmas gifts! You are the only one who has come to thank me, the only one? It is my pleasure to have you here Vince, you are a decent man and we appreciate you! My families have all heard about you and they are all astonished at your natural integrity! Tell me Verkerk asked why do you ride everywhere on a bike, you are very highly paid? Because we can't afford two cars Vince replied, my wife and I have two Sons now to lug around so naturally she has our car!

Verkerk one day asked Vince to work serving in the shop, in spite of not speaking Dutch. When asked why he answered because you will learn the language in no time, and he was right. Customers used to line up and wait for Vince to serve them so they could hear his accent. Many were the customers who congratulated Verkerk for the Dutch speaking Kiwi, working in his shop.

Vince had been there for about two years when the Foreman Burt, who had become a friend to him, died suddenly. He was only thirty five years of age, and he was killed by a blood clot to the heart. Two months after

Burt's death Verkerk offered the Foreman's job to Vince, much to Vinces' surprise!

How Vince asked do you think I can control a lot of Dutchmen? They all think of me as a foreigner and just want to laugh at my funny accent, when speaking their language? Sometimes they make me angry with their silly laughing!

You will control them easily, because you are the best man here for the job! Burt was too easy going and the men knew that, but they won't get away with anything with you. We (Verkerk Family) want you in charge because we all believe in you and your integrity, even my Wife is one of your supporters. We don't do anything important without having a vote on it and you have been selected. Then he quoted the full time wage Vince was to be paid, and that was it, Vince accepted and was the new Foreman for a Dutch firm!

Very quickly Vince had learned all of the work done by the company, and there was no difficulty controlling the Staff? He had also achieved his dream and became a highly skilled meat professional. His depth of knowledge with a very wide range of Meat Processing, hands on skills was unique. Dutch and German smallgoods' are very similar, so Vince was proud he had the knowledge in three systems, Kiwi, Dutch and German.

There was only one thing that was being kept from him, and that was the secret formulas'! The formulas were kept written on a wall in Dutch! Verkerk didn't know it, but Vince could read Dutch so that secret information he now had as well. When he finally left Verkerks it was to work for himself, and he had gleaned most of his knowledge, from Verkerks, Cross Bros, and the Meat Works! Within twelve months he had built a big business using that specialized knowledge.

Meat Contracts Christchurch

1962: #35

Meat contracting is a highly specialized job a lot different than the retail industry!

Vince had set up his new Company Vinads' Ltd and had been extremely successful, in the first two years, he had won several major clients and they were all very profitable! He had decided to quote for the Christchurch Hospital Board meat supply contracts these were renewed every six months, and were usually won by either Cross Bros or Verkerks. Fortunately for Vince he had been the Manger of both firms and while with them, had got to know the dietitians at all of the seven board controlled hospitals! In deciding to quote, Vince knew he would get favorable reports from all of the dietitians, just as he had from the Hotel Chefs and Restaurant Owners. Before he put in his quotes he lobbied all of the Dietitians, especially Mrs. Rees the one in charge of all of the Hospitals!

Bill Cross had been a friend for some twelve years, so to be courteous Vince rang Bill and spoke to him before he put in his tender. Hi Bill he said it's your old Buddy Vince here, I want to buy some meat of you here is an order. Whats that you will be very happy to supply me, of course you will we are friends' and I bought your old dump off you as a favor? Whats that you know how busy we are, well that's good isn't it means we will be able to pay you as per our contract?

By the way Bill I am thinking of putting in a price for the Hospital Board do you want to do a deal with me and share them 50x50%, you don't why not? You think we will get burnt because the hospitals are too hard for

186

amateurs, even smart ones like me? That's not very nice, ok guess we will have to take the lot by ourselves whats that Bill? We will go broke because we aint got no money! Yes we have Bill we have yours, what more do we need you have plenty of money! Crikey that was not nice he slammed the phone in my ear, should we ring back, no let him cool down first!

Over the previous eighteen months Vince had bought Bills old Factory of him, and had promptly taken a lot of trade in the city away from the other two major meat companies Cross Bros and Verkerks? His Company had become a major player in the meat wholesale industry, and was now recognized as an equal to his opposition! The only thing he had not done was to take the hospital contracts, now those were being tendered for as well. When the new tenders were opened Vinces' company Vinads,' had won all of the contracts so he was now the biggest wholesaler, but with the oldest premises!

Aalt Verkerk one of the opposition firms rang Vince to congratulate him, but asked that Vince desist from producing Bacon and Ham using his formulas' in Christchurch. Vince agreed but stipulated the agreement applied only to apply in Christchurch the rest of the country was to be available to Vinads'? Bill Cross was very angry and never commented; many of his friends had told him he had been a fool to sell to Stephens! It would have been cheaper they said to bulldoze your old place down than to sell to that black barsted Stephens, he will tear both you and Verkerk to pieces, before he is finished?

Bill had tried to laugh it all off, but with the hospital contracts now in Vinces' hands he could no longer deny the truth! Vince for his part felt Vinads' was just legitimate competition, and there was nothing wrong with what he was doing. He would keep on doing it until he had the lot, Bill Cross he said had been offered a compromise, and turned it down so to hell with it he (Vince) would take the whole town? This is what he proceeded to do including buying another Continental Smallgoods Business, and backing it into wholesale, against Verkerks? This was a legitimate move and a very successful one, but to keep faith with Verkerk they only went retail and never used the Verkerk formulas.

The rise of Vinads' from nothing created a sensation in the meat industry, a North Island Maori was challenging the old stars Cross and Verkerk! Verkerk when he had started was ostracized because he was a Dutch immigrant now here was this Maori Immigrant; this was a terrible thing to happen? They would rather the Dutch Man than this young up start this situation was very serious.

A few days later the Chairman of the Christchurch Master Butchers Brian Shackle came to see Vince, what he asked are you doing tearing the industry apart! What do you mean Vince asked, we are trading freely just like you do with your fancy shop in the city, whats the difference anyhow? How many Lambs do you sell a week Vince asked? Well we sell one and twenty per week, but ours are all quality not like the rubbish you sell said Brian. Your fancy lambs would be considered as rubbish by our customers, if we tried to sell that stuff we would fail very quickly? My staff work twice as hard as yours because I lead the way so again whats your problem anyhow!

And how much net profit you make out of your lambs, Vince asked? Well about five dollars each Brian said but that's because ours are all top quality. Well we sell up to eight hundred sheep a week here and we make ten dollars each, so what is your problem we are charging a profit double than you are, it's you the one prices cutting not us. Let's not get into beef pigs and smallgoods because the result will be the same, you are under charging not Vinads'. Go back to Bill Cross and his friends like you, and tell them the truth we are doing the right things, it's just we are better operators than you and your ilk goodbye Mate!

A new car for his Birthday

Shit it's just a bloody car so what is all the fuss about anyhow?

It was Vince's Birthday 25th Oct 1965 thirty years of age; he was going home from Auckland to be with his Wife and two Sons. The NAC flight landed at the Harewood Airport and surprise, his Wife was waiting. She had driven out in his birthday present a Rambler Rebel American Motors car, top of the range and very expensive. "This is a bit costly isn't it where did you get the money?" He asked.

"Off our Accountant and why expensive aren't you worth it? The Accountant says you are making heaps of money so what a few thousand pounds? Then she said it was tax deductible so a possible argument was averted. Vince was to have a few incidents in that car that he thought was funny.

When he was home in Christchurch it was his habit to make sales calls, this time was to be no different His first call was to a major manufacturer who had never given him an order even though Vince called regularly, all he had ever got was, "Hi Vince how are you today?"

This time when he walked in he was greeted with, "Hi Vince, you must be doing well for yourself now you look as if your company is affluent enough to supply us?"

"What you mean the car? My wife bought it for my birthday, to me it is a waste of money, but she says its tax deductible so that means it's not so costly really. As far as me wanting a new car it's just a waste of money, but how do you deal with a wife who makes up her own mind. But my damned Accountant should be fired for telling her how well the company is doing!

"Well let me help you to pay for that car, as far as we are concerned now you look good enough to supply us. Here is an order can you supply it? I often wanted to give you an order but that old car you drove put me off?" He said handing over an order requisition.

Vince looked at the order and replied, "Of course we can supply this order, thank you very much. Why does the car mean so much difference anyhow, we are no difference now than before. I hear what you are saying about appearances, but surely it's more than that.

"If we place an order of that size with a supplier, I have to be confident it will arrive. Now to me it gives a confidence that wasn't there before, he said with a smile.

The next day Vince was going into Christchurch City and on the way, he was stopped at a crossing waiting for pedestrians to cross over. An extremely attractive young Miss was crossing and as men will, Vince had looked at her in a casual way she must have misunderstood.

The lovely Miss at first ignored him she was obviously well used to men's hopeful looks, then she noticed the fancy car. She turned and almost stopped walking and gave Vince a brilliant smile she obviously liked the car very much. Vince returned the smile but drove on, he had no interest beyond a look or two, nothing more.

Still in his home City and in his new car, he had to drive into what is called the Square. He drove over to the side that in those days was the only area with parking, pulled up and stepped out of his car.

He was taking no notice of anyone or thing until a Sergeant of Police walked up to him and rather belligerently asked, "Where did you steal that car Maori Boy, show me your license and registration papers, now did you borrow it while no one was looking?"

"What do you mean where did I get this car, where did you get those three stripes you have on your shoulders?" Vince asked in an extremely threatening manner. "Now Mr. Police Sergeant don't you dare call me boy, what do you think I am an American Negro? What say we go to the station you work from, and lets you and I have a bet. I will bet you will lose those stripes quicker than they take this car off me. A racist dumb copper in Christchurch well how about that?" Vince said with a nasty sneer.

The Sergeant turned on his heels and walked away, grumbling to himself something like struth a smart Alec Maori how about that?

Vince arrived home a few evenings later and there was a very fancy Ford Futura Sports sitting outside, gee that's nice thought Vince as he walked inside. Wander who the visitors are, must be important with a car like that?

When he entered the house there was no one there, but his Wife so he asked, "who is the visitor and where are they?"

"What do you mean visitors, there are no visitors here?" His Wife asked in surprise.

"Oh the car why that's mine, you didn't think you were going to be driving a fancy car while I drove around in that old Zephyr did you? That's my new car isn't it nice I picked it up today and it's beautiful to drive, just as nice as yours. Would you like to go for a drive?" She said with a big smile.

"Well let me tell you a car like that for you isn't tax deductible now is it, and does that stupid accountant know you have it?" Vince snarled very angrily, "I will fire him for sure if he does know? This is the most expensive way for you to get a new car, buy me one first. Hell I am away 70% of the time you could have driven the Rambler while I am away.

Meat contracts Vinads' Auckland

1968 : #37

Vinads Auckland had leveraged the Hospital Board in Christchurch and had won all of the Auckland Hospital Board contracts as well.

Vince had bought a big factory in Auckland about ten times the size of his Christchurch property, and they needed more work to make it viable. The freezers had a holding capacity of five hundred thousand tons and that space was all needed, for Xmas stock and to serve Birds Eye? Special machines had been imported from Germany, and Kiwi and Continental Smallgoods' could be produced at the rate of one ton an hour. Two contract boners were full time employed, with a total staff of just over one hundred and forty including a few women packers. The staff numbers in Christchurch was only a total of thirty!

The Birds eye contract plus a trial order from Watties used up various cheaper meats', Hotels and Restaurants took all the prime cuts. T/Bones Rump, Scotch Fillet and Sirloins were all sold to Hotels at double retail price, the reality being only big producers like Vinads' could supply the volumes. All fillet steak went to Air New Zealand at three times retail, and all Topsides, Rounds and Silversides went to Birds Eye also at higher prices than retail?

This left the processing meats about 33% of the beast going to clients like Hutton's of Australia and Kiwi Bacon at a little cheaper than retail. To improve those process prices, Hospital Contracts were needed because they could be blended to improve all profit margins including cheap meat cuts. The aim is to sell the full meat range in bulk but achieve at least retail prices.

This was how Vince had fooled all of the opposition in Christchurch, he knew how to blend the meats and achieve full profits? The big failure was not having a big farm as most other big operators did, but that was next on the agenda!

Vinads' had bought fourteen shops in Auckland, and named that company Ngapuhi Retail Meats Ltd. Vinads' was also packing Bacon and Ham for the big Auckland retail company Shoprite, owned and run by Wally Morris and his family? The only sales missing was Hospital and/or Govt Contracts. As he had done in Christchurch, Vince went to the current contractor and offered to share the work, but once again was rebuffed? Vinads' tendered for all of Auckland contracts and used the Christchurch Hospital Board as a reference? The result was Vinads' won the Auckland Hospital Board all of their twelve big contracts, Army Camp at Papakura, Navy Base at Mechanics Bay and the Royal Air Force at Whenuapai?

Watties canneries had put in a trial order; Birds Eye had ordered one hundred and fifty tons to be delivered as soon as possible. Finally the Vinads' Group was in balance! There was a special Continental shop and Pre packed Frozen Foods as well as Vinads' in Christchurch and now that had been duplicated in Auckland, Vinads' was really stirring up a hornets' nest of anger? It was from then the opposition really wanted to take Vinads' down in both Cities, but especially in Auckland Vinces' home town.

The really big problem was that Vince had now created a company beyond his skill to control; suddenly a big administration was needed. Dalgety's had tried for a takeover bid? The shops were not performing as expected, in fact well below profit margins they should have achieved, for the first time in his life Vince was in strife? Try as he might he couldn't bring the whole Company into administrative balance, he bought in a Management Consultant and he just made a mess, but charged thousands' it was really tough going?

Administration was not the fatal flaw, it was the failure to control theft from the Factory by Staff that in the end killed Vinads'? The foreman of transport and his brother, conspired with Vinads' opposition to steal frozen meat out of the freezers, and in the end it was just too much? One of the biggest Public owned meat works in Auckland was at the same time a victim of massive theft, and they also collapsed under a mountain of losses.

Vinads' could have been saved there is no reason to think they could not have pulled through! Personal and tax problems broke the drive Vince had, for the first time he could not face everything that was going on at the same time?

It was claimed by somebody he trusted, that the Tax Dept was after him for Tax evasion, and that the Police was after him for fraud! At the same time his marriage was breaking down, and his Wife took away his Children that was the straw that broke his spirit.

Some years later he was speaking to a complete stranger in Australia NSW; a Northern Maori who when Vince identified himself laughed! Out of curiosity Vince asked the stranger what the joke was, and the stranger said I have known you for years, but you did not know me! He then proceeded to sketch out a plan of the Vinads' plant in Auckland NZ much to Vinces' astonishment, how Vince asked did you know all that?

Well it was like this the stranger said, years ago my gang was commissioned to break your hold on the Auckland market, but we were not told to send you broke! It was us that organized all that theft, and we used that driver and his brother to do the job! When we heard what happened your opposition was real happy, even though we are all from the same tribe up in North Auckland as you are? We had not meant to send you broke just break your grip on the whole town, it was obvious you had them all beat on straight trading?

The ironic part was that the Insurance company got away without paying the claim on the grounds the thefts where done by staff. Finally the proof was there it was organized by criminals, the claim should have stood. It was real hard for Vince not to break down and cry.

A Farmers Beef

The trick in any business is to buy low and sell high, not like this effort!

It was sale day at the Christchurch sale yards and Vince was as usual, buying the cattle and Pigs needed for his business. He employed an agent to buy his sheep because sheep and lambs were sold at the same time as beef, pigs were not. Vince had become well known at the sale yards, Christchurch is a small city and the newcomer was a Northern Maori. Sadly back then the men from the North Island, had created for themselves a bad image, none realized the bad ones were just passing through! Christchurch was a temporary stop off, for work men travelling to Balclutha and Invercargill, in the Deep South of New Zealand? As Maori men will Christchurch was the place to stop off and party, after the overnight trip from Wellington on the Ferry Boat? Conversely there were men arriving from the South, and celebrating the end of the seasons work. Vince had not been able to get over the North Island born tag!

The South Island born Maoris' had a southern accent and was accepted, the dislike was not for Maoris'! It was against Northerners and Vince was one of them? The fact that Vince had settled in Christchurch and setting up in business there, was a further insult, unfair but real? From his point of view staying in Christchurch was his Wife's choice not his! Vince was ready to shift north to Auckland at any time, and he would have been happy to leave and never stopped in Christchurch. They had arrived first place 1956 when he and his Partner had first come together as a pair, and had somehow stayed.

Vinads' the firm jointly owned by Vince and his wife, had come from nowhere very quickly! The experience he had, allowed Vince to be very competitive by reducing his wages costs, and other expenses. The finance for their factory was very cheap and his equipment although old was highly functional? Vinads' could produce all of the products Vince had learned to make, especially from Verkerks'.

It had been the usual sale dominated by three firms Verkerks, Cross Bros and Vince for Vinads'? At the weekly sale it was usual for Vince to compete against the professional buyers, working for the two larger firms and all of the small buyers? Vince was hated at the sales by the small firms, because he had stopped all of them buying for themselves! The small operators could not keep up with the buyers, because they were not able to calculate values and weights of the cattle quickly enough? Professional buyers liked Vince because he had got them new customers who could not compete, and so had to employ them and pay commissions?

On the day we here refer to, it had been a good sale for Butchers because there was a big yarding and prices were cheaper. After the sale had ended a Grazier, (Dry stock Farmer) came up to Vince and asked if he wanted to buy a herd of beef cattle. This was attractive to Vince because he had not yet learned to buy direct from the farms, this was his one big disadvantage. Both Cross and Verkerk had farms and bought most of their needs from other land owners! Doing this avoided paying commissions to the professional buyers, and the stock and station agents. Vince knew it was only his cost controls that gave him the advantage, and he had to improve his buying systems to increase the profits of Vinads? He agreed to go out to the Graziers' property, and sight the cattle then offer a price!

Verkerk always came to the pig sale, and Cross always came to the sheep and lamb sales. Both of them were very good judges of animals, so Vince had no advantage when competing with them. Both men even though Vince was a strong competitor to them, and a friendly relationship was obvious, between Vince and his two ex employers?

Arriving at the property, Vince transferred to the Graziers' car that was the first mistake? Next mistake was the time set up by the Grazier, it was in the evening, and as they drove into the paddock they were looking into the setting sun? The cattle he was being offered were pure bred Black Polls, and they were standing beside a fairly low white timber fence? The fence made the cattle to look bigger than they really were; the animals looked at least twelve months older, than they were. Vince was to learn a lot about buying on that first attempt, here is how the trap was set and carried out on that expensive first evening of trying.

First was by going into the paddock in the Graziers' car, he had no control on the way they drove towards the cattle, the Grazier deliberately drove into the sun! Next was looking into the sunset it was harder to see the real weights of the animals he was looking at. They were magnificent animals enhanced by the sunlight. The white fence made the beasts look bigger white behind black and into the sun! As the Grazier drove towards them, as cattle always do they stood up and stayed in one place facing the car being driven towards them.

These cattle will weigh out at three hundred and twenty kilos at least said the farmer, Vince a good judge agreed and based on that a price was negotiated. Then the Grazier offered to sell twelve hundred grown at a price, but in this offer there had been no smart tricks. When the weights came into the Vinads' office, the cattle averaged twenty five kilos underweight, so that was a big loss over one hundred and fifty animals! The sheep were a good buy and in this purchase Vince was happy. The methods' employed by the Grazier in pricing his cattle was an experience, that was costly and not forgotten ever by Vince.

Company Mentor

To Vince the best Mentors he ever had!

Vince and his wife were watching T/V one night when there was an advt; came on for Birds eye frozen meals! Look Vince said to his wife that mob has to buy a lot of meat from somewhere, and it may as well be off us, I will ring them tomorrow. He did ring and was told yes they buy a lot of meat, and they would have the buyer in Hastings ring back the next day? The buyer Dudley Williams did ring and arranged to come to Christchurch, to negotiate with Vince for Birds Eye to buy meat from Vinads'. Dudley came down within about a week! This was the biggest customer that Vinads' was to have over the years, and Dudley Williams became a long time friend! Dudley had to inspect the Vinads' plant to check they were capable to supply Birds Eye? Vinads' was quickly approved and a week later the first order arrived, an order for one hundred ton of meat delivery within ninety days? Vince looked at the order scratched his head and thought crikey this is a little bigger than we ever imagined, one hundred ton that's really big time now, can we actually do this order? After thinking about it for at least twenty minutes he thought sure we can and signed the acceptance, this doubled the size of Vinads'.

The battle was on immediately, the cry went out for more cattle Vinads' needed another one hundred head of cattle per week, which was the first problem! This was the first time that Vince realized that sometimes over demand, created cost increase over the full account? The next problem was the extra capacity squeezed the factory and plant so hard, that costs also blew out and created extra variable costs? Wages did not as expected come down, they could not, the rate of efficiency was so effective they broke through that efficiency, and wages also blew out?

Something had to be done and fast there was only three months to fill the order, and one month was gone already, what was to be done? At the time Vince, Wife and Sons' were going away on holiday including going to Auckland Vinces' home town? That was wonderful he would leave it all alone for a while and figure out how to deal with a serious problem when he came home.

While in Auckland he did come up with the answer he bought a very big shop, with a large work area, and started production there immediately? The shop cost him ten thousand pounds cash, and this time there was nobody to screw, he had to pay cash and straight away! He did buy the shop and they did complete the Birds Eye order by diverting it from Christchurch to Vinads' Auckland a new company.

It was another dynamic move, Vida Auckland promptly became the Auckland equivalent of its sister firm in Christchurch! As if from nowhere there was a new major meat firm in Auckland and the growth was even more spectacular. Once again the orders flooded in, but now there was Birds Eye taking up the cheap processor meats and there was a lot of prime cuts for Hotels etc? This meant the cheap cuts and now the prime cuts were all sold, but the medium cuts needed an outlet to balance sales.

And so it was off he goes again, but now it was getting dangerous, at that level of trade a top administration was needed, and Vinads' did not have that? Vince was a top meat man, but his big mistake was he did not know how to build an administration, in the end that was his failure? Another one hundred ton order came in from Birds Eye and now there was no hesitation, that order was needed but for Vinads Auckland? None of the order went to Christchurch! Auckland is a beef province and there were plenty of cattle, pressure in Christchurch went back to normal!

Vince was now moving from Christchurch to Auckland every week, and he was working in Christchurch on the Monday. Then he was flying to Auckland on Tuesday and working there until Friday when he would fly home! This was a tough routine, but because he was used to being on the run it all worked, and now he had become as big a challenge to local firms in two provinces?

It is a common procedure to pump water into the meat, to shorten up the time it takes to freeze, and this was done with the orders for Birds Eye which was all frozen meat. The danger is if it takes too long to freeze, the meat that is unfrozen may get lower in the stacks, and not freeze at all. Even though the new plant in Auckland, bought off Fletchers for over one hundred thousand pounds, had the capacity to hold five hundred thousand tons of meat, it still wasn't blast freeze? To counteract that water was pumped into the fresh meat, and that speeded up the freezer process considerably!

One day Dudley Williams rang Vince and said, the meat inspectors here want to know why the blood in this beef is so light colored Vince, can you explain please? Yes sure said Vince immediately, it's because we are sending all heifer beef and they are young animals, of course the blood is light colored, what do those blokes expect anyhow? Dudley rang back a half hour later and said, our inspectors agree and are very happy we are getting heifer beef keep up the good work mate! Oh by the way we will be increasing our orders next time to one hundred and fifty tons, our people are very happy with Vinads' and are approving you as our main supplier! This was at that time the biggest meat order for local supply in New Zealand and Vinads' had the lion's share, not bad for a Northern Maori who started with nothing but his wits.

An old bomb car in Sydney

1971: #40

These coppers in Sydney they be real smart, no wonder the gangsters always win here.

Vince had arrived in Sydney and of course had no car; he had managed to save enough to buy a pretty bashed up Holden HR. The car looked like a bomb, but was in good condition under the bonnet and that was all that Vince cared about. Who cared what a car looked like, it's like a woman once the paint comes off, whats left is what you get he used to think.

There was a need to take the family into Sydney, so it's into the old HR and off we go. The old car was covered with country dust, the last week out in the bush the roads had been very dry and dusty. Should go through an automatic wash machine on the way into town, but what the hell next week will be the same dry and dusty, so whats the difference? Anyhow if the dust was washed of the old girl would look even worse, but she was a beauty out there on those long dusty roads.

A park was found in Pitt St. at the Central Railway Station end, and Vince was just getting out of his car when he was accosted by a young single stripe copper. "What are you damned Kiwi's doing here in Sydney the young policeman asked, why don't you lot go home and stay there we have too many of your lot here? Look at that car it's a disgrace take it away and dump it.

"Crikey Mr. pleeseman man boss but it be berry good here ya no. We comes here getta da dole more dan in NZ it berry well here. Sleep all day on

Bondi Beach you Aussies pay me ebery weeks why go back to NZ I not silly like sleep all day get pay berry good.

"You Kiwis' are disgusting and yes we pay you the dole our Government is stupid all right? One day when I am in Parliament I am going to vote for Kiwis' to be barred from our country we don't want you." The young man sneered. "One day when the Government wakes up to the Kiwis' in this country, we will vote to send the lot of you home in a canoe, yes that's what we will do and on the way we hope you all drown. And we won't even come out to the rescue we will let the whole lot of you drown, yes that's good let you all drown.

"But me donna want to go back no like da canoe no waan drown swim berry good might swim back Aussie berry good yes boss man. likea da dole here me stay sleep on beach sleep every day women at noight dis be a good country orright no me be gonna stay at boni beach for sure me stay fer a berry long time. Maybe soon dey moight increase da dole den me stay forever. That be good den I be an Aussie to, what you tink bout dat Mr Copper?"

I think it's a disgrace you Kiwis' are just bludgers on our country that's what I think, there should be some way you could be sent back; and refused entry ever again. One of these days we will export the lot of you back home that's what I think," said with much anger.

We have people from all over the world here, but you Kiwis' are the worst lazy, stupid, dirty, drunks and dole bludgers that's what they are. We think the Wogs are better than your lot, at least they work and, they don't bludge on us even if they all stink of garlic. They are good people not like the Kiwis'.

"Well now you fine young Copper, here is what I really think just so you know. First there are way too many Australians going to New Zealand, and bludging on our small country, some Kiwis' have an attitude like you. Next my fare was paid for me to come here by sheep farmers, who can't get enough good shearers here. You might like to know we earn more in a week than you earn in a month young man. This car is used on the roughest roads in the Australian back blocks, and only an idiot like you would have a flash one. Finally idiots like you are fairly rare over here; we mix with the real Aussies out on the land, not you townie bludgers. Now young man, buzz of unless you have a charge against me because you make me sick. Thank God there are not many like you here in this beautiful country, you are real racist shit. You are just a young semi literate fool, and I am a University graduate, now buzz of before we report you for hassling decent citizens'?" All said with total clarity.

After being so chastised our young policeman wandered off completely stunned, gosh how do we figure out those damned Kiwis' he was thinking. They sure are a weird mob; I wander if what that fellow said was true.

He was to find that yes many Kiwis' came to work for employers who were paying their fares, mostly contract workers like shearers and meat men. There are more Aussies living in New Zealand than Kiwis' living in Australia, this is natural since the difference in the population sizes is quite large. More Kiwis' than Aussies pro rata are University Graduates. New Zealand originally was largely settled from NSW, and the ANZAC means Australia, New Zealand Army Core. To top that off he found that very few Kiwis' stayed in Australia on the Dole, the ones that did were at Bondi and were short time visitors. It was the Bondi visitors that left the wrong impression of Kiwis' living in Australia. That young policeman soon changed his attitude to Kiwis', but he never ran into Vince ever again.

The Receivers

Maurice Teague of Christchurch were the accountants for Vinads in Christchurch and Auckland.

Mr. Stephens your accountant in Christchurch is on the phone can you take it on line two; will you take it now please?

"Yes Thanks, hello Maurice what can I do for you today?"

"Vince what the hell is happening, I have just been served notice of intent by Dalgety's they want full payment of 200,000 pounds within 24 hours or they are appointing a Receiver. They have asked for a meeting in my office tomorrow at 10am can you be here."

"Yeah I guess so but make it 4.00pm don't want to jump to high for them do we? Oh and Maurice stop the panic it's not so bad the Hospitals owe us 300,000 pounds and there is over 200,000 pounds here in frozen stock so settle down."

"OK it's all up to you, but they seemed pretty determined to me," replied Maurice Teague the Vinads group long time accountant.

What a pain thought Vince oh well I guess I have to fly to Christchurch in the morning, that's a nuisance, we have a pile of work here without this.

Vincent rang the Dalgety's agent and asked, "what the hell is going on with your mob, so I owe you 200 grand so what?"

This is no joke Vince, Pritchard (Dalgety's CEO) wants to take over Vinad's you are our biggest buyer at the sale yards, and he is concerned you may shift your account can you pay us? The Prince is banking on you not being able to raise the cash in such a short time. If you can't Vinad's is going to be the new meat division of Dalgety's, but it's ok he only wants 51% he wants you to stay on as the CEO and 49% shareholder."

Vincent to Mr. Pritchard, "and what precisely are you up to now so you want to take away my company is that right?"

Hi Vince, "no not quite but your company is very important to us we want to ensure the account can't be taken away. Vinads is buying 50% of the livestock going through the sale yards through us and we want to secure that position. But remember this, you will have no more money problems and you will be a wealthy man, it's not many men your age can be offered such a deal by Dalgety's we are a worldwide firm, don't be too hasty."

Vincent calling Maurice Teague, "I am running late Maurice, tell those Dalgety Fella's I will be there soon OK."

"Fine Vince it's not 4.00 yet how late will you be?"

"Oh just late enough to irritate them Maurice don't worry it will all be fine. See you at 4.15 that should be enough to set them of balance I think"

"Hi Maurice sorry I am late everything ok?"

"Yes I guess so but the Lawyers from Dalgety's are in my office waiting for you."

"Oh to hell with them let them wait they are only bloody flunkies for the Prince typical lawyers they mean nothing to me anyhow."

"Ok Vince but let's just get it over with now this is all making me very nervous."

Accountant to Dalgety Lawyers, "Gentlemen this is Mr. Vincent Stephens, and he is here to meet with you as requested."

Vincent, "Yeah well let's just cut out all the rubbish shall we, I can't be bothered with all that now what can I do for you."

Looking a little flustered one of the Lawyers said, "We are authorized by the Head Office of Dalgety's in Auckland to collect a cheque for the money you owe them and we require the account settled in full."

"Yeah so I haven't got the money so what are you going to do?" asked Vince.

"We have authority from Dalgety's to be appointed as Receivers to Vinad's Ltd, our mandate is to take management control effective immediately," smiled the senior honcho. "Please consider this action as being in process now"

Now you two Fella's just listen to me," Firstly I wouldn't let you manage the toilet at Vinad's, I doubt if your management skills would extend beyond this office door. The second thing I have to tell you is that I have today served notice in the equity court Auckland of my intent to appoint a voluntary Liquidator to Vinad's, as you know this supersedes your new found authority. Lastly go back to the Mr. Pritchard "the Prince" and tell him he has today lost the Vinads account, unless he just shuts up and behaves. Now screw up that silly paper you have there and throw it away."

"You can't do that," wailed the legal one, "I am the manager now of Vinads I have the authority here, just you read it that's on Dalgety's authority."

"Well you and your mate and the Prince can all kiss me in the sunset together or in tandem I don't care, but take that silly piece of paper and you can jam it right up Pritchard's rear end."

Now one final message for the Prince here is what will happen.

1/ Vinads as you know will be put up for auction.

2/ it's a voluntary liquidation so we have more than enough money to pay all creditors.

3/ Vinad's Christchurch will buy Vinads back off the Liquidator and start again because we will have no debts. The only change we will run the business from here

4/ Then the Dalgety's Board will sack both you and Pritchard for loss of the Vinads account. We will transfer our full account effective immediately.

5/ So now what have you got to say about all that Mr. Lawyer man

Postscript:

Vince Stephens won that battle but lost the war. Dalgety's were right if he had taken their terms he would have instantly been a very rich man. Oh well fools are a dime a dozen.

Pakeha Son in Law

Bloody Pakehas' ya can't trust the barsted's especially with ya Daughters.

It had been a disastrous day at the surgery; shortage of staff and doctors, inability to service pre operation commitments. Vince's temper was running very short, but having just arrived home the next shock he got was the biggest of the week. The door opened and for once, a usually taciturn (today demur) daughter Maryanne, looped her arms around Vince's neck kissed him and said, "Hi 'Dad how is you?" Three quick thoughts flashed through Vince's agile mind, Mary never jokes the language, she's very excited and she rarely shows her Dad how she really feels, so what the hell is going on here'?

Hm, there's an unpleasant surprise here for me reasoned Vince what's the catch, my Daughter has a surprise for me that's for sure, and it's not going to be to my liking. 'Then the fuss became obvious a large human object, was blocking the view into the family home in Blacktown, and it was standing about three metres behind Maryanne'.

"Dad" Mary chirped with a decided glow in her voice, "This is Mark Craven, Mark this is my Dad." 'Vince managed to step forward, shake Marks hand grunt, hello then escaped into the body of the house, to be met by his beaming wife'.

"What is that object out there with Mary," growled Vince, looks like one of those over height Yankee basketballers only this one's white where the hell did she find it pray tell me, did she steal it from the Zoo?"

"Don't you like him?" asked a badly deflated Wife.

"I didn't say I don't like him, I said I don't like the look of him still I guess with him around me I won't be the ugliest in the family anymore?"

"No you don't, not this time," beamed a reassured Wife, "this one's for real she's got it for real this one and she aint going to let him get away."

'Let him get away, you have gotta be joking if he turns out to be a dead loss, big as he is I will help him on his way and I for sure aint likely to improve his looks believe me," snarled Vince'.

"You can't help yourself can you?" squeaked Wife.

In time even Vince became beguiled by Mark's silver tongue and sound thinking capacity, reassured Vince. 'Mark became a Son in Law in which any father could be proud. At the wedding Vince expressed doubts about anyone taming Maryanne, but he didn't tame her he blended in with her, now that's smart'!

The years were good and soon after a Son was born Nicholas Leslie Craven, when Vince saw how gentle that big guy could be he was astonished. Here was a man who was a better father than Vince had ever been. One day when visiting, little Nick (now three years old) and his father were out deweeding the front driveway edging, Mark was happily pulling weeds and Nick was helping. Vince walked over just as Nick was putting a lump of dirt in his mouth; and looking set for either dinner or a stomach ache. "I don't think that's supposed to be eaten little Fella," said Granddad. Mark just turned to his Son stuck a big finger in the little mouth hoiked out the dirt, admonished again with that big finger, look Daddy said no and continued his work.

This was the first time Vince began to understand his lack as a father, watching Mark perform as a real father was a testing period, but hell it was far too late to change what had been, is an unchangeable truth. The trouble for Vince is the memories keep flooding back, but we know 'one must never look back with regret'.

As the end approaches there is no pleasure in looking forward reminiscing is one of only a few realities left, (pleasures) one cannot look back in regret else one destroys a life of memories, many that are a pleasure to remember."

'In the case of Mark, Mary and Co; the memories Vince has are among the many pleasurable ones.

Their Love for each other has risen above a problem that for many would be a disaster, a mountain many couldn't climb. Like a lot of families a son that is rebellious. Vince is aware of this problem, but it's private and controlled. It's great to watch these two real hands on entrepreneurs, and know that whatever their future they can deal with the problems.

The family has flourished; the work ethic hasn't detracted from the children's well being in any way all except one has flourished. Truthfully this one case is beyond their or any other parents, who are without professional knowledge to deal with this type of difficult problem.

Joshua 18, Caleb 15, Nick 8, Jesse 4, and Vince is starting to see Joshua's problem is really just a adolescent one.

The ugly in Vinces mind only ever referred to Marks size. Vince was envious of Mark's height, but for sure size or not Mark aint ugly now. Vince likes to think that maybe his Daughter helped turn that Drake into a Swan, or is it Goose he can't remember. Vince does know Maryanne Craven and the children are terrific, healthy happy and flourishing and Mark has done so much to create this situation, he is a great Dad.

When Vince heard Mark was going to have his Dad as his best man at the wedding he was deeply impressed. Now that's a wonderful Father and Son relationship. When asked why he had his Father didn't he have any friends? Mark had replied.

"Oh yes I have many friends; some since school days but none like my Dad," Vince laughed with admiration. That's not ugly, man that's beautiful.

Milk @ Supermarket

<u>1998 (# 49).</u>

Sometimes we wonder if our kids are really ours or if some neighbor dropped by, while the old man was at work?

It had been an interesting trip out to the farm, it was like a journey back into his memories for Vince, but his friends were all Australian townies born and bred. What they had asked, do cows and horses do? They (three Youths) were aware that horses ran in the races especially at the Melbourne Cup and all of Sydney stopped for that event. They had also seen the police riding horses in Sydney City, but they had never seen any use for cows. Vince had been highly amused on unobtrusively hearing them talking, and had offered to take them one and all for a visit to a farm on a teaching trip. One had offered the knowledge that we ate pigs cos he had seen a pig's head in a butchers shop, Another talked about lamb chops and T/bones although he did not quite know if a t/bone was off a sheep which he said was far bigger than a lamb. All were quite happy with the notion of learning what a cow was there for, and what about goats what use are they?

Vince had explained to the boys that meat for our local butcher shops came from all of the species mentioned except horses and Goats. Horse meat he told them was exported to Belgium from Australia and Goat Meat to countries' in the Middle East. Lamb and Beef went to America and many other countries worldwide, and that the three main meat exporting countries were Australia, New Zealand and Argentina. In was quite interesting to Vince too because he knew that in New Zealand, being small all of the youngsters were close to the land. Australia and the Argentine being so big the town folk did not know much about the country, and the farming community.

Sheep meat was an important protein in the Middle East, but they want the older animals because their cuisine is different to other areas of the world. The soft lamb meat is not wanted because they don't eat roasts' and BBQ style foods' They also eat a lot of goat meat, but those animals are not farmed in the three meat countries in great numbers as yet, but numbers are growing. The carcass features of Goats' are very similar to sheep and are processed in the same way.

Australia by comparison to New Zealand was an extremely difficult country in which to be a farmer of any type, the reliability of rain is an important factor. When there is plenty of rain in Australia it's so beautiful, but when there is the all too often droughts; it becomes such a harsh landscape. Australia has also diverted away into being a major minerals miner, and is no longer extremely reliant on agriculture. New Zealand has no minerals, therefore still relies on its agriculture, but their meat crops of Beef and Sheep meats is the best in the world. New Zealand is also in the fore front of Agricultural Science.

The Argentine has had a severe problem with Foot and Mouth disease that for some years, until the disease had been eradicated meat sales dropped steeply. If that disease or any other was to hit Australia and New Zealand, especially for New Zealand the results would be catastrophic. Live export of aged sheep and heifer cows in calf (pre milker age) to the Middle East India and China, has become a major sales for both countries. China and India are especially interested in buying the Heifers' because of the improving life style for their huge populations. Many of the Peasants' are now affluent enough to drink milk instead of water, and the impact will grow as the improvement becomes more wide spread.

The Argentine is even more restricted than New Zealand with a heavy reliance on Beef, and some sugar and grapes. The Renault car company in Argentina had unsuccessfully tried to set up a car manufacturing plant which was being shut down. The larger populations of Australia and The Argentine, compared to NZ means in many ways NZ has the advantage of being small. Unfortunately the loss for New Zealand of its main market for Lamb meats the United Kingdom in favor of the common market countries mainly France, has been a disaster. New Zealand was in severe Recession from 1974-1993 and has converted a lot of its sheep country high lands to the growing of radiate pine. The Argentine does have fairly good mineral resources, which have not yet been mined, because it does have political instability that has held that country back.

On arriving out at the farm in Aberdeen Northern NSW the boys were excited to see a lot of new born, up to two month old calves' first. A big herd of black and white Friesian cows were going into the milking shed. Vince had deliberately set the arrival time to be during milking, and the session was in full swing with twelve hundred cows to be milked. There was also the stink of newly cut insulage that is, what only can be described as very smelly for town folk.

Wow said one of the youngsters why are those things hanging down there? When told they were being milked one of them said, oh so that is where milk comes from, I always thought it came from the supermarket. And said one of the others those red cows and the other colored ones we see out in the paddocks, must be where chocolate strawberry and caramel milk comes from. Gosh said another now we know how important cows are, my Mum has those different types of milk in the fridge all of the time, so does mine chorused the other two.

Stealing in A&NZ

2008 (# 52)

~~These two Countries are thicker than thieves an industry that prevails in both!~~

The greatest trait Australian and New Zealand people have in common is in being thieves. My comments here refer to NSW and Auckland, but since NZ was originally settled by quite a few from NSW it is easy to assume that's where the common habit comes from. It has been my misfortune to be a major victim in NZ and then to come to NSW and find myself on the other side, in straight language as being a thief? As I write these short stories from the past it has hit me just how much was really lost when thieves sent me broke in 1970. First and foremost was my children, we can assume that part was rectified in part, but it will always be a blight on the memories. The business empire that had been built as I remember now was spectacular, and if nothing else this old man can be proud of the memories, he went very close to beating the established norm over in NZ!

Strangely it was his own people that (Ngapuhi Maoris') in the end defeated him. Sadly he was never able to recover, all he has done since then has been to make one mistake after the other, but his wonderful children do shine through as his quiet pride. His Grandchildren only add to the joy that is now his to savor! The record of his own life as a thief is well left behind and should be forgotten, but in the process of the telling one wonders where the truth really lays, who is the thief he asks? In his own case was it the insurance company that turned down his justifiable claim, the thieves who planned and executed the thefts, in NZ and then profited from the chaos they created. In Australia was it himself and his gang of thieves who committed the crimes, or the police, lawyer and magistrate that took his bribe money, it's on this basis this short story emerges.

The realization that major theft had been committed at his plants, both in Christchurch and on a grand scale in Auckland was the start of a life that went badly astray! In terms of money values in 2008 the thefts in Auckland were on a grand scale over two and a half million dollars, in Christchurch probably in the two hundred thousand class, but that one is a guess. In Auckland we had precise records of the value stolen, but that was only a small part of the total loss. The value of the business destroyed was in the high multi millions and my guess is at last one hundred million, probably more. One can argue that from such tragedies comes character, I find that prognosis silly there is a limit, to the human ability to absorb and benefit? Like all things in life extremes create negative opposites as it did in my own case, I in turn became a thief and a good one, because we stole millions?

Since I did meet the abominable character who was the architect of the thieving in NZ over in Australia, and have discussed him in another short story, its suffice to say we met in Long Bay jail. I was there for about two hours for a traffic offence, he was a guest for many years, I pray he is still alive and enjoying his free board in NSW? Yes long may he live, and may God chastise him in the future! He was the one who was instrumental in the demise of one of the oldest and biggest meat Public owned works in NZ, Hellabys that company was a byword in the meat trade, but thieves killed them to. There was no wonder Sir Hellaby died of a broken heart.

Now my own guilt as I see it, because guilty I am, there is no doubt about that. It was quite strange really I got involved quite by accident if such a thing can be called an accident! From that chance meeting and the semi trailer loads of hot meat coming down from Queensland, so hot it must surely have been half cooked on arrival, my own thieving career was started. I was not a beneficiary of the meat from Queensland my partner was, but that was my own starting point.

At the thieves invitation it was me that turned our own activities into organized crime, because it was only me who had the knowledge to do so?

It was also me that when we got caught who organized it so we could pay of the Magistrate and the Police; in today's money say fifty thousand dollars.

The crimes were highly organized; the victims were Jewels, Coles and Franklins food stores all over Sydney, and down South as far as Kiama. The major beneficiaries were the small stores that bought the truckloads of loot at cheap prices and the store managers who were in on the heists. And of course there was my own and the teams pay offs, but being thieves they were also money wasters, everything they were paid was squandered?

The victims over here were the insurance companies because that was my real payoff, not the trivial amount of money I personally received, that was not enough to feed on, but it cost the insurance companies millions. We were never involved in the use of weapons, unless we are talking about tools for break INS; the breaks had to at least look genuine with no staff involvement. Oh we made sure the break looked real; we made sure the insurance company had to pay the claims that was my dividends.

It gave me a lot of satisfaction to see the product going out and to count in my mind the enormous cost to the insurance companies it really did; I had become as evil as them. We were all evil Me, The Cops, The Magistrate, The shop managers for Jewels, Coles and Franklins, the Receivers and finally the actual Burglars.

Oh and yes the Insurance Company that turned my legitimate claim down, long may they suffer.

Working in A&NZ

Memories of yore is all we too cling too in the end.

New Zealand when Vince was young work was abundant and sales overseas were booming! The creation of frozen food shipping of cheap frozen meat from Australia and New Zealand to the United Kingdom was the start of major employment for the masses. The farmers suddenly had a market for their lambs and beef, butter was also a major trade commodity. Meat processors known in NZ as Freezing Works sprang up all over the country! Australia was to develop along a different pattern than NZ she built smaller works, more suitable for their huge land mass? NZ being far smaller and compact tended towards the very big works, this in turn created more seasonal work, thus was created the itinerant Maori seasonal worker moving from works to works? The first load of frozen meat (4500 Lambs) left Dunedin in 1882, pioneered by two Kiwi Entrepreneurs! This first shipment was a great success and frozen meat was now a reality for Australian & New Zealand future trade with the World.

Two years previously (1880) shipments left Australia and Argentina, but were not too successful, the quality was not really up to English standards? It was this fortuitous start that gave NZ the reputation it has had since then, for superior quality beef and Lambs, but a lot of hard work has gone into maintaining that reputation?

Auckland with its mild temperatures started the Lamb season in early Oct and finished in February! The Bay of Plenty started in early Dec until March, and the Southland Otago works started in early January and lasted

216

until early July. The different provinces in NZ produced different meats for killing! Auckland and the Far North produced Lambs, Beef, Pigs and Horses; The Bay of Plenty was mainly Lambs and Beef with a mass of horticulture. The South Island was more Lambs, with Beef mainly going to local consumption, Pigs were only grown far more up into the Canterbury Plains region.

Men like Vince started in Auckland for about eight weeks, then Hastings for another eight weeks and finally down to Southland for another six months. At the end of the Lamb season Vince transferred to beef boning, his season lasted from October until August ten months. Most of the travelers were Maoris' and they were normally away from their home province for at least six month, then two months at home?

Accommodation was supplied, most of the works had military type camps, and the food had to be fairly good to keep the men coming each season. Rugby, Gambling, Booze, and Cooking done by the Maoris' in the camp, was the only recreation! There were very few females around, areas like The Bluff with a total population of four hundred used to get at least one thousand Northern Maoris' in the season? The lack of females led to a few problems which gave the Northerners a bad reputation in the Deep South. Christchurch, and Wellington further north did not attract many travelers they were not in the season cycle.

Australia had a different set up than NZ, they developed a lot of small independent meat works, and the lower yield per acre there meant far greater distances to travel from farm to works? The methods back in the mid 1970s left NZ far ahead because of the large works being able to draw from closer high production farms to service their large stock needs to keep those big works going.

In NZ there was a seasonal grading of lambs in each province! Taking Auckland as an example, lambing in May thru July and lambs ready to kill in Oct, the grade would change from Lamb to Hogget as soon as the two teeth were thru? In Australia Lambs not having two teeth in the Australia wide end of season would be classed as a lamb for the next twelve months? This meant that in some animals they had four teeth and were still being graded as lambs, by the end of the following year! The writer has seen full mouth wethers being cut up as lambs for export to the USA; it was no wonder Aussie lambs were considered a bit tough?

On average even in the South with the larger breeds, NZ lambs would kill out at top weights of fifteen kilos' average! The Aussie down cross lambs were killing out at twenty five Kilos' and almost needed false teeth to eat the dry grass over there in the Dubbo area. The conditions in the inner areas like Dubbo and its dry surrounds in say Warren, when the shearers hit the belly opening cuts of the fleece it is like trying to open up concrete? Those plurry sheep some of them have never felt rain, when working on Kiwi sheep it's like opening up butter, Australian sheep buggers the hand piece in no time at all.

The waste of feed on the Australian product with an excess cover of 25 Millimeters fat on the carcass, when one is growing say twenty thousand lambs per season is easy to calculate. The drop in value per kilo is another big loss, the Kiwi lambs were selling back in the 1970s at a 15% premium and the UK could not get enough of them?

The loss of the lamb meat markets when the UK joined the Common Market has meant a very hard period for NZ 1974-1992, big acreage once running Sheep and Lambs is now growing Radiata Pine. The time needed to grow lambs for market of 4-5 months, is a little different than seven years for the first cut and eighteen to twenty five years for full grown Pine trees?

Australia with its huge mineral resources has very big natural advantages over NZ! In the area of natural agriculture though NZ has few peer areas anywhere in the world? Travel down thru the Waikato and the Bay of Plenty, and then take in Blenheim and the Canterbury Plains for farming. Up the West Coast in the South Island and up in the Far North for Tourism, there in none to beat it. We have not even written of Rotorua, Taupo and The Wairarapa?

But its home sweet home isn't it I almost forgot, I have been in beautiful Australia for so long!

Mum and Winty

July 1953(# 55)

Memories of the heart last forever, and so it has been over the last 54 years.

Mum was dying and Winty felt lost, only she and Aunty Claire had been close to him from the time he was born. There was his Aunt Anne to, but her husband (Owen) really disliked Winty because he thought Winty was a smart Alec, which was probably right? On the other hand Aunt Claire's husband was Winty's' hero and was like a father in every way? Mum had tried to adopt Winty (she was his maternal grandmother) but her Daughter's husband would not agree this had led to a lot of sadness for everyone until Winty got older. As the old lady laid breathing with difficulty she and Winty's eyes locked and the love between them could be seen by all of her children who were gathered around the bed? Mum was a small feisty full blooded Maori woman who had married a full blooded Pakeha! There had been seven children and the family had been a great success, the only failure was the death of the eldest son at WW11 in Europe? There were two surviving Sons, but both were war affected!

As he stood watching his loved one, memories of their past times together started to flood back to Winty, in spite of the difficult time it was hard not to laugh.

One day his Nan had come to see Winty and her Daughter it was a time of rationing during WW11, because Winty's parents had a small farm and business, they enjoyed having most rationed products as much as they wanted? Mum had been loaded up with illicit goods to take home, Cream, Homemade Butter, Pork Meat, etc; the old lady left with her big basket fully loaded. They went to the bus stop and Mum got on, but because she was loaded with goods she refused to move to the back and sat next to a fussy looking woman, about the same age. The cream spilled and ran out onto the ladies dress, she started to scream! Look what you have done you silly old Maori, you have spilled cream all over me, get out of this seat and bugger off you old fool. Where did you get

that illegal cream anyhow, bloody silly Maori, you have no brains at all. Old Mum could only speak pigeon English, but she understood every word the Pakeha woman had said so she replied. You Shuta up you silly mouf you maka me plurry sick, if you no be careful me wilt spill da rest over you silly head, Pakeha fool you be? I no shift da seat fo yu not me not fo yu anyhoo, I wanta bash you real good but no good you be cry lak baby no yu shuts up now u go sits back of bus now.

As she told us much later what had happened we laughed so much we nearly peed ourselves. Mum and Winty were traveling in a bus to the suburbs and a Pakeha woman got on the bus, she wanted to sit in the front and demanded Mum give up her seat? Maoris' she said were not allowed to sit up the front (There was no such rule) they had to sit at the back?

Mum who was a very small woman, stood up and said, I shifta moi seat fo no one's special u you be a silly old fool now go away fores I basha yo silly head silly old Pakeha u be crazy ting plurry fools yes? The Pakeha woman then turned to the driver and said, I demand you put this Maori off the bus right now if not then you will get a complaint for me at head office tomorrow and I will see you get the sack. The Driver looked at the Pakeha then at Mum and said, Lady don't ask me to get into your problems, she looks too tough for me there will be another bus in half an hour why don't you get of an wait for that? Then Mum really got going, you silly Plurry Pakeha you wanta puta me ofa da bus, you just stay dere for minute me puta yu off real quick and I kicka that big fat bum you got so much bum needa two seata not gonna gib yo nuttin but just basha yo head, now me said so u bugger of quick now.

Another time we were walking down the street and an old drunk collided with mum, looked at her and said. You Maori get out of a white man's way when we pass, do you want me to send you to jail. Without any preamble old Mum walked up to the drunk, hit him with a closed fist then said, now you be right Mr. drunka man. You are a dirty stinky man and yo tell me to get out ob road, you buggier of yo old drunka mon no good not even fo is Pakeha now shut up plurry ting. The old fella got such a shock he sat down and looked at mum and said you just assaulted me Maori how dare you. Yes Mum said an I be dares agin to yo want some more plenny mo here she said showing her fist.

Mum had three big Sons and Four Daughters all far bigger than her, size never mattered to her she was used to being the boss. Her Husband knew just what an incredible woman she was when he married her. They had been a great family the nine of them, ten including Winty. Mum couldn't say Vincent the name came out Winty that why he was known for years as Winty, but he didn't care she could call him anytime with any name?

Well now the old lady was dying and it was time to say good bye, Winty could take no more he leaned over and kissed his old Mum goodbye and left? Never has he been to her grave he left Auckland soon after for the last time and never went back for fourteen years, he just could not face anymore.

The Meat Works

1955-1960 (#59)

Meat was the industry in which Vince even in old age still claims to be an expert.

The meat export industry has been very major one in Australia and NZ from the start of the 20th century, until major changes in world markets with the start of the Common Market. After WW11 the two countries and Argentina could not keep up with demand for meat! Most of the work was done on contract or as it was more appropriately called piece work basis? Maoris' were of an ideal temperament for this type of work, Shearing and Slaughtering piece workers had a very large Maori contingent in NZ, and many were enticed to Australia by offers of free transfer costs etc. Maoris' tended not to be liked by the Australian workers initially, because they had the tendency to work as teams which was not part of the Aussie methods. In the afternoons in NZ the boards (so named where the work was done) would resound with singing as the teams broke into voice to ease the boredom, this was a common method of relief. One voice would start and the others would start up until the whole board was almost like a dance hall, or a big party with no booze? The harmonizing, of the around one hundred men was beautiful to listen too; sometimes even the few Pakehas would join in and have some fun with their Maori work mates?

Vince used to love these singing sessions to him it was like a party cos he only ever drank water at parties anyhow. At that time he was very young so was often the one who started the singing at Ocean Beach anyhow, but all works with a large Maori contingent were the same? The other thing that was different in NZ was the work man ship where each man made sure of the quality of his work! This meant a better quality of finished product, but to be fair the NZ lambs are softer than the Aussie product, and that's just caused by the rain, Kiwi sheep get a bath almost daily. When Aussies visit NZ they will always ask why the sheep are so white, when at home they are yellow, that's why Aussie sheep never bathe?

Aussie sheep sometimes never feel rain for their entire lives. To make it even harder, the lack of rain means Aussie sheep live with dust and flies so their skins are unwashed and carry the dirt from the day they are born? When its lambing times in Australia and NZ it's also the first bath time, in Australia it's a dust bath in NZ it's a rain bath the difference to the meat is vast.

Vince will never forget his first sheep in Australia, he didn't take much notice just swung his hand piece into place and took the opening cut. Crikey the damned thing bounced back, so he took another swipe same result, the bloody hand piece went sideways in his loose grip. Then he took a real hold on his hand piece and guided the blades in, but it was a shock for a while until he got used to the difference.

The really big difference is that Maoris' are very versatile they learn to do the full job and can move easily from job to job there are many different jobs when on the piece work system? The Maori will very quickly be able to do multiple jobs, the Pakeha will stay in one job day in and day out, and the boredom doesn't seem to affect them. Vince could never figure it out, why he asked are the Maoris' condemned as dumb, when they get so bored when doing the same job all day, that's why they learn multiple jobs. The Pakeha is supposed to be far smarter, yet he can stay in the same place doing the same thing all day no problem, it's all very strange indeed?

When the lambs or whatever animal is being processed are finished they are washed and weighed off with the scales adjusted to allow for loss age of 5% as the carcass dries.

From the animal apart from the carcass comes Tripe, liver, kidneys, sausage skins from the intestines, wool and or leather from the hides, bungs for bigger sausage, gelatin, blood and bone manure, brains etc.

The smelliest job in the meat works is the wool pullers, that's when the skins are ready and the wool can be pulled off, my goodness that is real stinky! That job is worse than the dirtiest job Vince has ever tried to do and he has worked on the night cart in NZ, none smells as bad as wool pulling.

Pigs sound almost human as they were killed, before the electric stunners were introduced. Sheep and lambs are real quick and they don't feel a thing. Cattle and horses are far harder even when they are stunned goes down on its knees the equine (horse) rears back on its hind legs and can be dangerous. The goat is the same as a sheep they are small animals so go quick and easy.

In the meat works when the Jewish Rabbi or the Muslim Sheik come out to get their animals done for Kosher Meat, it's very slow and production is cut by 50%? They make the special cut to start the bleed and then I think say a little prayer, but the carcasses are then kept separated as required, and can only be delivered to kosher shops.

The men have no idea what the ritual is all about and often abuse the holy men, for being in their words bloody nuisances. If you speak to one of these slaugtermen you will find they have nothing but contempt for the practice, it is considered by all and sundry to be very cruel? Vince has watched it being done and agrees it's bloody cruel and should be done by their own men in their own premises, it is not a practice that Christian males like to be forced to watch, and even worse participate in.

My Brother in Laws

1969 (# 60)

I like my brother in laws really I do, but I don't think they like me either so it's a fair exchange!

It's funny I never had much time for my two Brother Laws Graham and Eddie two dick heads or that's what I thought! When I was in Auckland back in 1969, it was Aloma crying Graham has gone off on a binge again. Or was it Eddie he is on the piss and Maria hasn't seen him for a week. As for Ngaire her blokes in jail and that's the best place for him, but at least I didn't even meet him thank God! Susan well she was just a kid then anyhow, but she grew up and gave her bloke a Maltese dick shit, a hiding that's what I was told, but I wasn't around by then. But hang on those blokes are still married to my Sisters and I have been round the marriage game several times, so since when do I have the right calling them names, I need to think about that?

Everywhere we go now it's oh that Graham is a great guy ya know he works so hard and brings his entire pay home to Aloma! And Eddie well he is a paragon of virtue and a church leader, my God what happened to me I am still running around chasing my tail, it's a crying shame it be. Its true only God had the right to judge his children, cos left to me those two would be dead meat years ago, but my Sisters are happy now and that's what matters isn't it?

We grow old and we get wiser well at least those two did, but it seems some of us miss the bus, and I must have been one of them who missed out!

225

It was years ago when we went, Cheryl and me to visit Eddie and Maria in Whangarei, and we went to church together. They are Seven Day Adventists, and during the meeting it was my place to wash Eddie's feet, hell I thought wash your feet many is the time I have wanted to smash your head, sorry cant think like that in here can I? Here feet take that from Vince and God bless ya feet. You are all right feet but why don't you fall over with him and bust his silly head, oh sorry about that feet. Now feet you is nice and clean feet, but whats in the head feet is it still full of booze, no it can't be his eyes are not crossed anymore, no you is pretty good there now feet? The Adventists is smart all right you take everything out and blame the feet praise, God and good on ya feet!

Now that dick wit Graham, where the hell is he Aloma I am going to Kill the basted, you what? You still love the silly looking prick, I will give him love all right let me bust his bloody head. Look at those two beautiful kids you have got there Aloma, and he is running around like a single man, I will give him single man let me kill him I tell you he is a parasite he is, can't even feed his wife and kids, he is just so thirsty? Don't worry about him running off with another woman, no he won't do that none would have the ugly barsted. No that's not a problem at all no not at all, believe me only you is so cross eyed you think he is beautiful, no but he is bloody ugly Aloma let me say it again Darlin he is bloody ugly, he what he is beautiful? You have shit in yo eyes Darlin he is ugly let me assure you o dat.

I will guarantee ya sis he won't run, no he won't worse luck I wish he would run away just wish the prick would vanish! How did you get such beautiful Kids of that lump of shit did ya jump bloody fence did ya Aloma crikey its miracle it really is? You know he should be in jail with his brother, isn't he the brother of Ngaire husband yes that right I thought he was!

Hey maybe he is off with Eddie on the piss somewhere do you think that may be it, no neither of them have other woman no not at all Eddies feet stink, I know had to wash the rotten things ya know they is ready to go on strike they won't him to wear his socks to church with them, I washed them and put a hex on his feet just so ya no?

No I will never wash Grahams feet he needs to get them looked after to cos, he is probably runnin around with no socks on as well, pissed as parrots both o dem.

I dunno my Sisters are all beautiful where did they find these men and what about Susan yo have to be an example to yo little sister, we can't have her bashing her man up now can we it's no good for our reputation Ya no it's not good Aloma not good at all? Susan needs to keep her fists to herself ya no we can't go round beating up on Maltese's ya no they is respectable people don't ya no dat is yes they are respectable those Maltese, a bit like Maltese terrier dogs they is ankle biters not back biters no not at all I said ankle biters I know dat's dem Maltese terriers sis.

I will have to go and see Susan she is a bully fancy beating up on a Maltese Terrorists that's a terrible thing ya no they can only bite ankles ya no, it's not good our sister she beat em up no she will have to be told no more o dat beating up the Maltese's it be no good at all.

Well those are my Brother in Laws they be good blokes ya no but I aint going to dat church any more, let Eddie wash his own bloody feet that what I say anyhow. I grew to like my In Laws but like me dey is getting old now, so they don't run off they is like me to can't be bothered?

Rugby Trials

Break a boys Spirit, be a bloody idiot.

Winty had been chosen at his Seddon Tech Memorial College for the North Island Schoolboy Rep trials! He was so excited he had, had a terrible time settling into college, and to be chosen as a rep in the game he loved was beyond his wildest dreams, he was ecstatic. The college coach had been so complimentary telling Winty he was a natural, and should make college rugby captain by year eleven. The game he had said was more than just brawn, it also needed brains and Winty had a footie brain, such compliments Winty was starved for, he was so demoralized.

Since coming to College there had been a series of disasters, it had started when he was second in the entry exams! Teachers and Parents had loudly claimed he must have cheated, this had been proved wrong by producing previous exam results, from his primary school! There was a history of academic achievement as a youngster, but when he got to College that all stopped now he was treated as the local clown! Winty normally loved to compete at anything, but at college this trait he had which had always been strong was quickly quelled!

Then on the day he had started the other kids would not sit next to him in the form room because he was a cheat so claimed by their parents, and confirmed by the teachers? The only one of the teachers who treated Winty with any semblance of respect was the Math's teacher, but then Winty always had a math's brain, respect would have been for that reason only?

He had on his first day at physical education been ridiculed in front of his class peers as inferior, because all natives were physically and mentally inferior to Whites? This was claimed by Mr. Rees the phys-ed teacher! Winty had been bought up to the front of the class and after being told to remove his singlet, Rees demonstrated with a ruler why he was inferior to his class mates physically? Then Rees had, using the same ruler showed by the shape of Winty's head why he was mentally inferior, as well and had no capacity to think like the other White Kids? This Rees claimed was why it was a travesty for Stephens to be allowed to sit in the presence of whites; Niger's said Rees should never be allowed to sit when whites are in the room. Stephens should therefore not be in the top stream class as he was? This had been accompanied by sniggers from the class who were asking questions, mostly as to how Stephens could have cheated and why!

All of this Winty had to endure while beginning to for the first time in his life feel totally inferior, he had always been praised as superior! It did not take long to kill Winty's self respect, and he hated them all for what they were doing to him! Jimpy Powell the A grade form teacher, took electrical science and Winty hated him and his classes, Winty's brain just closed down and he was demoralized! Jimpy made it very plain he did not really think any Maori could learn his subject anyhow it would be a waste for a Maori to be taught in his classes. Winty could have told Jimpy he had no wish to be a dumb arse electrician anyhow; college was for Winty a nightmare.

It was compulsory that the students do work practice, Winty was sent to a lawyer's office to apply. This was done by the College office and that turned out to be a nightmare as well. When Winty went in and told the receptionist why he was there, he heard her say to someone out back Seddon College has sent a Maori for work practice, what do I do boss? Ring that smart arse at their office and ask him what the big idea is sending us a Nigger, and tell them don't ever send anymore Niggers here? Oh and tell that Nigger to piss off case we don't take Niggers here, they stink! Winty slunk out of there like a dog that has been kicked, and he never went back into another office for years. Years later he was invited into the fancy office at Kiwi Bacon in

229

Christchurch and greeted like a man not a stinkin Nigger, but the memory of that day lingers on right up until the present day.

Anyhow the trials were being played; Winty's specialist position was in the centers, coming in to dummy half when the play called for it. Winty had been sitting waiting for his turn to have a run, and after about an hour he said to the coach, when do I get a run coach? You aint never gonna get a run in any team I coach you little Nigger Basted said the Coach! Even if you were not a cheat you still will never play in any team that I have anything to do with, now piss of you little black basted, I hate you fuckin niggers. They should have killed the lot of you years ago then we would not be having the trouble we are having now, go on piss off, I say. Winty left the field and swore he would never play any sport ever again, even though especially Rugby he loved the game, he was really heartbroken that day.

He was even offered to become a member at Titirangi Golf Club a most prestigious club and a great offer but he refused. He had been playing Cricket and Softball, as well as being a Champion on a Horse, but he even gave all of that up, no more for me he thought no one will ever speak to me like that again. Years later in the army at Papakura he was amazed and amused when the trainers were teaching and explained why the Maori physique is superior to the white man, touché Rees you old prick he thought.